¶

THE PARAGRAPHS

Praise for Rick Berlin

"From the mind of an artist, Rick Berlin's writings are as unique as his music. He continues to be a Boston treasure."
— Oedipus (WBCN, The Oedipus Project)

"Rick Berlin's incisive, fearless vignettes cut to the bone and then pat you on the back. Relentlessly colorful, necessarily detailed, and sometimes nearly unbelievable, Rick's life stories are vital and disarming and everyone should read them."
— April Greene, freelance writer

"Rick Berlin's writing is as raw, luminous, open-hearted, profane, musical, magical as the man himself. Put on your seat belts."
— Beth Harrington (documentary filmmaker, *The Winding Stream*, member of The Modern Lovers)

"Like Leonard Cohen, Rick Berlin's poetics are timeless. Speaks directly to the heart confronting us with postmodern mythologies."
— Amy Rome

"At the age of 70, maybe older now, Berlin remains a free man. His defiance toward most of the tired categories of social life that hem others in is a reminder of the superiority of soul and a goad to the rest of us to go get some more of it. As Rick reminds us, it is free."

— Christopher Mackin (Ownership Associates)

"I love reading Berlin's words. All the pretty young boys and girls got nothing on Rick. He can light up the darkest places."

— Carmelita (Bay State Rock, WAAF)

"Rick Berlin is the voice of the generation that had the best time in the Boston music scene, and he is our voice still. Singing and writing voice, that is!"

— Adrienne Wolffe Feddersen

"Rick's voice is so strong they read like a transcript of a monologue. The ones that struck me the most were the ones about him as a kid or a young man. Clues to how he became the man he is. But what I think I loved most about them is the feeling I get from a lot of Rick's songs too: Life is sad, but in that sadness are moments of joy and magic."

— Jeff Chasse (songwriter)

"Such a mix of street edge with the humanity of a poet, Rick Berlin carries his life, his music and his community close. He writes about unbearably sweet horrors and a longing that keeps burning."

— Jane Hudson (video/film artist, owner at Hudson ART, Inc.)

"I love Berlin's paragraphs. They allow me to escape from my pathetic life and slightly slip off into a place I rarely get to go. I enjoy reading every fine tuned word he describes in detail every aspect of the story. Shit man, he could write a story about going to the mailbox in pink flip flops and somehow manage to make it exciting and worth day dreaming about!"

— Tim Czifrik

"I have been enjoying Rick Berlin's paragraphs since his 'Ich Bein Ein Berlinner' days. Rick is a master of imagery. His vignettes of the human condition are at once raw and poignant. Rick's words stay with the reader long after a paragraph has been absorbed. His writing is succinct and powerful. This is a must-read, not just for fans of Rick's music, but for anyone who enjoys the art of thinking."

— Susan M. Vertullo

"Rick's writing comes from the soul. He's unafraid to be honest, raw and revealing, telling his readers – a hungry bunch who can't seem to get enough of him – about the in's and out's of life and love in all its complexity. And in doing so, he makes our own foibles just a little more okay."

— Mindy Fried (Co-Producer Jamaica Plain Porchfest, author of *Caring for Red*)

"Berlin's words paint such great pictures of what you see and what you feel."

— Marian Ferro (DJ - Rock Under the Radar)

"Reaching in, as Berlin's been doing, goes beyond your own experiences and helps to provide a map for others to do so for themselves."

— Bob Lewis (Owner, President at Video Visuals)

¶

THE PARAGRAPHS

rick berlin

CUTLASS PRESS

Boston, MA

Published by

Cutlass Press

5 Green Street

Boston, MA 02130

cutlasspress.com

ISBN-13: 978-0-692-80248-9

Cover and text design by Nicholas W. Kent

Dedication

To John Casey. A man who loved words and those who spoke
them with a true heart, who wrote poetry I never heard, and
who read 'IRISH' aloud outside the Brendan Behan Pub to a
friend. It never sounded more alive. Also, to those who speak
beautifully and never write a line.

THE PARAGRAPHS

what ARE these?

In order to have new song lyrics hit the page like bullets, I began writing 'memorabilia' word bursts. I'd dredge up an autobiographical moment or observation and write it down. Pictorial. Honest. Moving. Funny. Ridiculous. I called them 'paragraphs.' Grammatically they are nothing close: no indentation, e e cummings lowercase (unfaithfully observed). Darts on an ouch dartboard. The 'collection' metastasized over time so I thought it would make a cool book.

¶

BOYHOOD

"*It is always sad to leave a place to which one knows one will never return.*"
— *Gustave Flaubert*

"*Genius is the recovery of childhood at will.*"
— *Arthur Rimbaud*

JIMMY-DOODY

i was born in Sioux City, my sister Janie, in Tuscon and Lisa, in San Francisco (Dad made a lotta moves). we didn't actually live in San Francisco, but across the bay in Oakland. when i tell someone about my past however, i say San Francisco cuz it seems cooler. i remember where we lived, even though i was only five—a narrow, three-story walkup with carpeted stairs and a dark interior. i went to a school where you're supposed to learn immersion French. the teacher, when i arrived my first day, was cleaning piano keys with a damp cloth, one note at a time. boong...boong...BOONG! she never looked up. she frightened me (quivering lip), but i gutted it out. after school i'd walk home with a friend and we'd throw rocks through the windows of an abandoned house, set back from the road with an overgrown front lawn, a broken gate and rusted, discarded bikes: a freak landscape. a rock shattered glass, hit something weirdly soft and a howl curled up out of the depths, scaring the piss out of us. we'd run away shrieking and laughing, high on fear. i made my first best-friends out there: Jimmy and Judy ('Jimmy-Doody' we pronounced them). they didn't go to my school but we'd meet up in the afternoon and invent stuff to do. one day we pulled turds out of the toilet, wrapped them in tin foil and Christmas paper and tried selling them door to door to repulsed neighbors. our thinking: there was so much of it around maybe a fortune could be made (children have all the answers). back then my Dad had a pale, green DeSoto

4

with heavy, steel doors that made a sure sound when you yanked them shut. it had that brand new smell: leather and gasoline. we took her for a spin across the Oakland Bridge, which had a road surface of metal gauze—you could see the bay rippling below. Janie rode shotgun, i was in the middle when her door swung open, her small, chubby hand on the latch and half her body stretched away from the seat, one foot swinging like a doll's. i could see the blink blinking of the bridge girders flickering underneath. i grabbed her by the wrist and hauled her back in. Dad was screaming. as i picture it, as i tell it, i saved her life, but i probably made the whole thing up. a month later i swallowed a peach pit and couldn't 'go' for days. they took me to the emergency room. the doctor snapped on a rubber glove, smeared it with goo and pulled the doody out of my ass. Jimmy-Doody. i trace a lot of who i am back to that moment.

UNICORN HORN

as a kid, an 11-year-old boy, i found a single antler in the woods near our big, white house in Simsbury, Connecticut. it was a three-foot-long piece of smooth ivory, a twisted yellowing tusk. i knew it belonged to a Unicorn. it had to. there was no other explanation. i buried it under wet leaves and put a boy's spell on it for safekeeping. i told people about it but never showed it to anyone. finally, it was lost, or decayed into the ground or was absorbed into the ether—magic for sure. i still remember it like a favorite character in a book that stayed with me years later, or a lover from a dream too real for reality.

MISS ZABLOCKI'S TITS

my third grade teacher, Miss Zablocki, would stand behind you and gently lower her tits onto your shoulders, two warm, sleepy kittens against your neck, placing them there, it seemed, to encourage wonder and confusion. would tit A slide down your chest like pizza dough? would tit B shift and locate a bra-less nipple against nervous skin? would they smell funny, like sour milk? would they lift-off gradually or with a snap? did every kid in class, boy or girl, get the same pair of presents? we never got answers. we never talked about it. we held her in awe and mild fear. an angry Miss Zablocki would swat her hand on your desk so hard you jumped. if it hurt her too much she'd use your hand and smack it on the desk instead. whatever you'd done to piss her off you never did again. sometimes, to get your attention, she'd force the entire class to stare at the black board where she would draw a giant, chalk circle that zeroed in (a concentric spiral) like an old-fashioned Hollywood special effect implying 'vertigo.' you'd become discombobulated, nauseated and woozy. in better spirits she'd tell us about her travels abroad (i think she went alone). floating like balsa wood in the Dead Sea or playing Canasta on a card table in the Great Salt Lake. she maintained a seated position because the salt was so buoyant (this was hard to picture). she had dark, cherry lipsticked lips, bottom lip larger than upper, with a clown-like exaggeration effective as either smile or frown. when she castanet-snapped her fingers, the flesh under her arm jiggled like Jello (we covered our eyes). she was the first exotic character i knew. her wild, flame-dyed hair, trumpeting alto and exaggerated East European hand gestures were all first-time new for me. she walked to school on cold days wearing a loose, partially-buttoned, billowing blouse, her Spain-red hair writhing like snakes as her long-legged, high-heeled, tick-tock steps echoed on the pavement. big, loud women have scared the shit out of me ever since. third grade changes you forever.

STRIKE OUT

my Mom was in a recuperation house after having a piece of her lung cut out (T.B.). i was 11 or 12. because she was away, they thought it'd be smart to send me off to Camp Viking on Cape Cod. i made a model of a schooner with a sleek black hull. it actually sailed, which was unexpected and we went on trips in the real thing. we skinny dipped at dawn. it was an ok time, but unfortunately i was sick most of the summer and spent it in sick bay. me and another kid spotted a knothole in the wall that we pushed out on purpose so we could look in on the nurse's station. we would peek in and watch her undress. we never saw much beyond bra and panties. i wasn't sure about myself in the naked-girl turn-on department, but i do remember liking the shoulder of the other kid against mine as we watched with naughty excitement. not that we ever did anything, he and i. one night he decided that i needed a 'sex lesson.' he made me take off my pajamas. with a pencil and paper he drew a cock and balls and showed me how the 'white stuff' came up out of the balls and squirted out of the boner. he also showed me on me by touching my stiff little crayon with the eraser end of the pencil. i never forgot it. still, none of this was as critical or as shameful as the baseball incident. i didn't realize that i was a homo back then (who does?). what i did know was that i was a shitty athlete, even before Viking. there i stood on the field during batting practice one humid afternoon and this a few days before i wound up in sick bay for good. was there a connection? i stood at the plate, legs apart, bat cocked like a wet noodle and could not hit the ball to save my life. not even once. swing, miss, swing, miss over and over and over again until i was fighting back tears. the coach pitched meatballs and still i couldn't hit. 'you're gonna stand there, Kinscherf, in the batter's box and you're not getting outta here until you hit the god-damned baseball!' he yelled, level-eyed—a real man. i stood there shaking and crying and swinging and missing and swinging and missing. it was a horror show. the other kids stood around watching, scuffing their cleats. he didn't let them make jokes, but i could hear what they were thinking: 'faggot.'

STAND BY US

Stevie lived in a one-story shack—damp and mildewed and covered with grey, rotting shingles—with an absentee Mom and Dad. or maybe i just never saw them. he had boxes and boxes of comic books that we'd pull out from under his bed and leaf through, lying side-by-side on the floor, up on elbows like praying mantises. Stevie was poor, at least compared to us. we lived in a big, white, three-story house with lots of land, a horse barn (without horses), a swimming pool, a vegetable garden and 'help' ('two tons of it,' as my Dad used to say)—two fat women and a rail-thin, old man. Stevie was my best friend and it was only much later that i noticed the contrast between our houses and the incomes of our Dads. every afternoon after school, i'd walk over to his house through a path in the woods that stood between our proper-ties. we'd hang out, run around the fields, show each other our 'things' under the umbrella branches of a weeping willow and throw rocks at the trains that ran behind our houses. i don't think we talked much, but we were inseparable. Stevie had mouse-soft hair, cut close with an upturn at his widow's peak. he wore second-hand clothes and his fingernails were dirty but there was nothing insecure or apologetic about him. i think the favorite thing we did was pluck overripe tomatoes off the stems in our vegetable garden (which eventually died the slow death of neglect). we'd lick the skin, salt them down, bite into them with the juice and seeds squirting all over

9

our faces and smile that big smile of knowing that we both felt the same joy at the same time. it stayed like that—Stevie and Ricky—until Richard moved into town. he was the new kid—spry, handsome and soon to replace Stevie as the person i wanted most to be with. maybe this was my earliest glimpse of homo-love—although, i wouldn't have called it that. it was also, in a way, my first infidelity, the first time i can remember moving away from one heart attachment to another. one afternoon my grandmother caught Richard and I pulling each other's pants off on my bed. Richard left in a hurry. after we moved to Philly, we wrote letters, quasi-love letters to each other. when i think about it, Stevie and i were easier friends. we didn't share or require the love assault on our emotions. i'm not sure if he was hurt being upstaged by Richard or if he was hurt because i did nothing to quiet him or to repair our friendship. regardless, both boys played a part in my early life. Stevie by being the kid from the 'other side of the tracks' who didn't have a phony bone in his body and Richard by being the accepting object of my affection. they continue to live in my heart to this day. don't they all.

ZITS

during the hair-down-there transition, i got hit with serious acne: zits all over my face—crusty, puss-oozing mini volca-noes. all my friends, save one, were zit free. i grinned my way

through it, feigning obliviousness. weekly visits with
Dr. Savage (her real name) didn't do much good. she focused a
hot lamp on my face and went at them with a stainless-steel,
miniature cocaine spoon with a tiny hole in the center that
she pressed against a black head and popped the puss out in a
thin, wormy ribbon. if we were quiet enough, and god knows
i kept my 14-year-old mouth shut, you could hear the thing
geyser: a teensy pip followed by the faint hiss of mustardy
ooze. i wasn't sure how to handle this. feeling ugly on top
of wondering why i had uncontrollable erections when my
friends slept over did not make for an easy passage. meanwhile, i was in choir—at this point, with puberty, an alto. i
felt the glare of stares as we entered the chapel. one kid called
me 'pizza face' but Karl told the kid to shut up. they painted
out the crust in the class portrait, but you could tell. there
were tiny removal scars all over the gloss. i guess we're not
supposed to be reminded of our grotesque teen face way down
the road when memory becomes selective. every time i see a
kid who used to have that perfect peach complexion suddenly
show up with a pimple problem, my heart goes out to him.
seems to me that boys have it worse than girls. or maybe with
my predilection i don't notice. i actually think a zitty face is
kinda hot. maybe like heroin chic there'll be zit chic in
Details magazine.

HARLOW MY HERO

Harlow was The Man when i was a boy growing up on the Main Line, just north of Philly. he lived in the big house across a thin road from our big house. his family and mine were inseparably close until the inevitable college diaspora. we did small kids 'dirty things' in the fields when we were small. we built tree forts, hauled up buckets of pine cone ammo to heave at imaginary enemies and had school girl crushes on each other. but it was Harlow who was the undisputed king of our insular, one-square-block hood. he sported a floppy, white-man's -fro, had a lanky build, angular features, rarely needed a shave (though he was hardly baby-faced) and had a sharp tongue and flint-sharp eyes. he seemed to know all the post beats: Dylan, Baez, Van Ronk were his discoveries and he turned us on to them. he could play hard, finger-picking folk—none of his own songs, but the newly minted from the soon-to-be legends. one night, drunk, he sang 'Motherless Children' in front of my, at the time, best friend whose Mom had just killed herself (there were a lotta suicides in my hood back then). this didn't slow him down, forthrightness was his MO. maybe he did the right thing. he always seemed to do the right thing, even when it seemed 'wrong,' which shook up my pre-teen head. he did that a lot, shaking up the complacent and the fearful. word had it that he fucked Baez, but we were never sure. he scored big with the Bryn Mawr girls even before he graduated high school, which, near as i can tell, he never finished. he started his own construction company (in his early twenties) in South Philly, tearing apart brownstones and putting them back together and yelling at workers in a good-hearted way. a kid on the way up we figured. i worked for him one summer, in over my head, but his charismatic bluster held me in thrall. hell, he was friends with Mott, an inventor who looked like Merlin and met visitors at his door stark naked and bellowing. Harlow (nice name for a boy, right?) won the heart of an insanely-beautiful Russian girl, Leah. they had a kid. we were never sure if they married but there was a famous photograph by a famous photographer that showed Leah's full tit squirting milk on their baby and they let the kid ride Mama's back when they were fucking. at one point he accumulated a pile of parking tickets at his construction sites which added up to thousands in cash. he couldn't afford to pay them so he changed his name, skipped town and moved to San Francisco. he got a commercial pilot's license and flew rich people up and down the coast. the last great time we spent together was when my Dad flew him out to Santa Barbara to pick me up after i'd been busted and jailed for shoplifting. we drove home cross-country, non-stop, high on meth and solving all the problems of the world in one sleepless trip. i wonder how he's doing. breaking barriers still, i bet.

¶

FAMILY

"When my mother died I felt expanded, slowly, durably, over time. I felt suffused with her truth, spread through, as with water, color or light."
— Don DeLillo *(Underworld)*

RETURN TO SENDER

it seems, much as we fight it, that on many levels we become
our parents, especially as we get older. our bodies and per-
sonalities fun house mirror them both (Dick and Jane in my
case—their names, for real) and resistance is futile. i see their
legs when i throw mine up and over my head in the yoga
'plow' every morning. there they are, white as a flounder's
belly, my bowling pin thick and hairless calves with brown
spots the size of nickels from the sun, recognizable as both
mine and my Mom's. my under-chin, what's left of it, is strung
like a lazy hammock in a straight line from chin to Adam's
apple, just like Jane's. my heavily lidded eyes are chestnut
brown, squinting and ready to laugh just like the old man's.
my toenails are warped and twisted like Mum's (she retained
enough vanity to paint them, crushed and distorted as they
were, whore red). the back of my hands are thick-veined,
raw, spotted and crêpe-papered like hers. my belly, distended
and pale, lolls out in slow motion like a poorly-curled bowling ball, as was Dick's in his last days, dying of alcohol. like
Jane, i keep things neat and throw away anything i'm sick
of. like Dick i chase the young. like him i like bars and dark
adventure. like her i'm frugal and generous at once. like him i
never hide from a good fart. like both of them i love to laugh.
of course, in other ways i presume differences, but i'm closer
to the tree than i'd imagined. in my sidewalk-self i think i'm
young, smooth-faced and fabulously interesting. did they? i
never asked.

RIGGY

i spent the spring and summer of 1971 on Martha's Vineyard,
a year before band after band took over my life. 1971 was the
tail end of all the summers of love, which i'd believed in like a
hippie evangelical—mucho acid, psilocybin, peyote consumed.
in fact, on my very first 'on island' landing i was ripped. i'd
hitched down Route 3 with Pat and Sam. we got our last ride
on a 16-wheeler, got off the ferry and got a ride to Oak Bluffs
which, under the influence or not, looked like the Shire. the
gingerbread cottages, undulating in the LSD air, had to have
been built by Hobbits. we were looking for Toby. he'd been
in a motorcycle accident and was hospitalized. turns out, his
roommate was a lesbian pilot, one of seven from an all-les-
bian, pilot cove (no kidding—they flew the island in v-for-
mations). she offered him a house on a field in Menemsha—if
he'd shingle the roof, she said, he could live there until the job
was done. we add-on squatters took her at her word. in less
than a week, five of us moved in. we brought a 100 pound bag
of brown rice, kerosene lamps, sleeping bags and an upright
piano that we liberated from a church. we set it up in the
kitchen, banging away as Michelle cooked elaborate vege-
tarian dinners by kerosene light. it was our cartoon circus—
nudity, pot, booze and LSD taking center ring. this was gonna
be our fucking summer of love, brakes off. Michelle painted
a white bone on a slab of driftwood to mark the unmarked
dirt road that led up to the house. we got day jobs as painters,

working for a Portuguese boss who mocked our beards ('why grow on your chin what grows wild around your asshole?') but who went easy on us and our faux-Wavy Gravy lifestyle. we painted rich people's houses, high on ladders and drugs and listened to Joni Mitchell and Carol King on a paint spattered boom box. after work we'd gas up for the ride home and hit the booze and the drugs hard. the kid who pumped gas in town reminded me of that Wyeth painting, the one with the boy with that huge listening ear. he was from Indiana, a farm kid with yellow hair and overalls. he drove out to the 'farm' on a Vespa for one of our perpetual day/night parties. he vomited in the front seat of a truck when i went down on him and then he bolted. i never went back for gas and i never saw him again—it was that kind of summer. on weekends we'd drive to a fresh water pond, skinny dip, walk a narrow sand path from pond to ocean, swim in salt water where pebbles, shells and rocks looked like crown jewels, stumble back, rinse off in the pond, drive home, eat, drink and renew the cycle all over again. we were unstoppable, happy and wild on life. one clear-as-a-bell afternoon, i dropped, hit the pond, slipped on a pair of fluorescent flippers, slid into the water and pumped the circumference at what felt like 90 mph. round and round and round on my back, the convex sky rising above me in fish-eye distortion. back on the beach i heard my Dad yelling: 'Riggy! Riggy!' (how the fuck did he get here? how did he find me?). with my sister's high school friend standing beside him, he stood at the top of the incline, a styrofoam carry-all crammed with ice, cups, vodka and tonic in one unsteady grip. he'd been

dipping into this all afternoon while they hitched and drank
their way around the island and now, lo and behold, here he
was. SURPISE! he ripped off his shorts and plunged naked
down the slope and into the water where my incredibly high,
skinny dipping friends were treading water and grinning
hard-wired, Captain Beefheart-my-smile-is-stuck-i-cannot-
go-back-to-your-frownland, ear-to-ear grins. he seemed
overly real. he stayed a few nights at the farm, charming my
hippie roommates and leering at the broads. he walked in on
me one night as i was sucking some kid's cock in my bedroom,
flailing about in the kerosene light. he ducked back out the
door without a word. i shrugged and resumed. at dawn he was
spotted hugging his knees on a rock in the surrounding field
cooing 'whippoorwill...whippoorwill' as if the bird might land
on his shoulder. Dad let his freak flag fly.

COLLISION DOLL

at 14, we thought it would be cool if we could get cars to crash
at night, on a dark stretch of road near our house in Wayne.
there were nine of us: Henry, Harlow, John, Teddy, Lilian,
Keith and the three Kinscherfs. we made a life-sized doll out
of clothes and stuffing and strung a clothesline across the
street near a bend in the road that was surrounded by trees.
we dropped the line, lax with the doll looking like a ten-
year-old child, attached at the neck. we practiced. we would

abruptly yank the clothesline and the fake kid would snap to startled attention, performing like a marionette. we waited in the trees. it was past midnight and cool out, not cold—no shivering. we hid on either side of the road waiting for two cars—one from one end of the street, one from the other. then we heard them. we could see the headlights. we knew what to do and we knew how to escape. we knew the woods, the crazy property. as they neared, 200 yards between them, we snapped the rope and the fake kid popped up and froze like a deer in headlights. both cars slammed on the brakes. tires burned rubber and screeched to a slow-motion halt, but not fast enough to avoid cracking into each other. we heard the glass shattering, one headlight out, mad cursing from both drivers and doors opening and closing. we crept backwards into the dark woods and made our getaway, hearts pounding, sweaty, unable or even afraid to speak. we were pretty sure no one was hurt but that they might have been was a chastening thought. we stopped doing stuff like that afterwards. we never read about the accident or heard anything, but we knew, each of us. it was an unspoken secret. we lived, if for only a few frightening minutes, on the island of the Lord of the Flies.

FIRST FIGHT

i was in Weatogue, Connecticut in 1955. our house was a big-box, three-story, white-clapboard wedding cake with a wrap-around porch, acres of lawn, copper beach trees and a massive, untended vegetable garden. it was idyllic, miraculous and the least-disturbing part of my childhood, until late one night, after bedtime, when i got up to pee wearing flannel pajamas— no hair down there, watching the stream—shaking off until i heard something new: an argument in the kitchen. the voices thundered up the backstairs. i heard Mom, furious, her tears folded into the yelling. i heard Dad screaming back at her and a glass shattering. i tip-toed to the top of the back stairs and the shouting got louder but the words were either indistinct or i didn't let myself understand them. i hadn't a clue that my parents weren't ok with each other. just that afternoon i had helped Dad paint New Yorker cartoons on a bathroom wall (a rare collaboration). last night i had watched Mom get ready for a cocktail party in her incredible gold dress—'you look like a movie star, like Tallulah Bankhead,' i bragged (Tallulah's voice—deep, low and ironic—had captivated my prepubescent imagination, replacing the Lone Ranger in my pantheon of luminaries). but that was hours ago. this fight hit me like a rock in the head. i covered my ears and retreated to the back porch: a screened-in, second story 'day room.' there the sound was muffled. i was 'intrigued + repulsed at the same time' (as my friend Jane said once about seeing a strap-on for the first time). it was like finding out that Santa Claus was a lie. i took Mom's side in my little head. she was hurt. i should defend her. but was that fair? i hated hating my Dad. sure enough, a month later, things got worse. when he took me on a ski trip, i ratted him out: he was plastered, there

were women on couches in our bedroom laughing. One? two?
college girls? i wasn't sure. this was new. they were 'guests' i
supposed but they also seemed to be 'with' him in some way
i didn't understand. while i'm on the phone checking-in, i tell
Mom about it—the drinking, the girls—and right in front of
him, close enough to get smacked. he went berserk. he said
he'd never trust me again, his fairy-assed son. the little boy
he calls the Prince as in 'you pay more attention to the Prince
than you do your own husband.' and this after she refused to
call in sick for him at the bank—'you're hungover, you're not
sick. go to work.' i thought she was right, but i was never sure.
i was proud of how crazy he was, of how easily he could make
her laugh, how he liked to fart in the elevator and blame it on
a stranger. but i remembered that first fight and i wanted to
protect her from being hurt again, so i ratted him out, 100%.
i shamed him in front of his college girls and in front of me,
his son. i threatened his manhood. two years later on a train
from Philly to Montreal for yet another ski trip, we kids were
about to conk out in bunk beds, the clickity-clack train wheels
soothing us down, when Dad stumbled in, shattered and loud.
Mom clocked him one, a sucker punch to the jaw and he went
down. it had to be tough for a guy to get punched out by his
wife in front of his kids. i realized, deep down, that we loved
them equally. it was more painful to take sides than not, even
as we did, jumping from one ship to the other in hopes of
some miraculous balance. we are never certain where love lies.
we wonder if our subsequent luck or ill fortune in the relationship game grew from that fierce, unyielding Yankee tempest.

CUTE

'cute' applies in a weird way to my Mom, even as she's fighting lung cancer with chemotherapy treatments in Portland.
one day before her 77th birthday she tugs at the edge of her
wig. the tendrils of what's left of her hair peek out. i snip some
off. we laugh but i notice that fear shades her eyes from time
to time or a far-away, inward look as she drifts from our conversation. her trembling hands look up a number in the yellow
pages. her green-rimmed eyeglasses tuck under her wig like a
pencil stuck into a rubber bathing cap. her eyebrows (one bent
and lonely stalk here, another there) are sparser than ever. she
walks steadfastly away from the waiting room in her regulation, robin's egg-blue, hospital robe for an x-ray. she does not
look back. her wig is on right, but to her it feels as if it bubbles
up on top of her head, leaving an itchy cavity between her
balding skull and the nape of the wig. she applies herself to
this assault of lethal chemicals with what-else-am-i-going-to-
do-about-it-I-hope-this-works, matter-of-fact Yankee courage,
dread, hope and helplessness. all this is transparent in her
wrinkled face, the face which she finds 'so old' when she looks
in the mirror. tonight i catch a glimpse of her in her under-
pants and sunset boulevard turban. she says goodnight all
over again as she sees me seeing her, but she does not start.
she is not ashamed of her body, of her mottled skin, the testa-
ment to her ongoing battle with pre-melanoma. she is girlish
undressing for bed, caught like a snapshot in the soft light.

DOG FOOD

my sisters fried up a can of Alpo and told Dad it was corned beef hash, over easy eggs on top. a morning hangover 'breakfast surprise.' Dad loved it. ate the whole thing. the best he'd ever had. they never told him.

DAD 'SAVES' ME

i'm not sure i've got this right—selective memory colorizes and distorts—but here it is: Dad was playing tennis at the Club: 'the Club' was what they called the shingled, one-story building where you signed up for golf or tennis or watched Sunday movies or bought a lemonade or a sarsaparilla on your parent's tab; the Club was located near the magic-door entrance to Prouts Neck (home to Winslow Homer and many of the scenes he painted and a summer retreat for the rich and socially registered)—it's a beautiful, short-thumb peninsula poking into the Atlantic off the lower coast of Maine; it's where my Mom grew up and the locus of many first stirrings of the heart and of my imaginary world, including my first public performance on a piano—an upright in the hall at the Club where we put on end-of-summer spectaculars on a rickety, red-curtained stage. i played a faux-classical, self-composed 'piece' all by myself and was rewarded with room-papered applause. one mid-afternoon, as i skittered across the narrow, two-lane, sand-shouldered road in front of the tennis court where Dad was playing doubles, i was hit by a car. the speed limit, anxiously observed, could not have been more than ten miles-per-hour. i was 12, in shorts, no pimples yet, bright-eyed and probably on my way to see a dirty friend. i was knocked to the ground and scuffed my knees. it was no worse than that. Dad heard the screech of tires, flung his racquet, shot through the pine grove to my rescue and lifted me up in his arms. he was worried and red-faced angry. he was screaming at the driver who was probably someone he knew, or maybe not—it's unclear. but i know i was proud of him: proud that he rushed to my side, that he ripped that driver a new one. this was before the shit hit the fan with the wake of infidelities, the bottles of gin and vodka buried in the woodpile, the embarrassed, broken man he would later become. i had forgotten about this day, this sunny, blue-sky afternoon at 'Proutsy Proutsy' as he called it. the place where he was silently blackballed for his loud mouth and drunken insults. but he was so cool that day and my narrow, 12-year-old chest filled up with the sight of him.

GETTING OLD IS NO FUN

my father's brother, Uncle Karl, was one tough guy. he was an athlete who played football for the Giants and held the punting record there for decades. he was a soldier who, during the war, drove an ambulance for the American Field Service in Italy. he was a fly-caster Rambo who broke his leg a mile from his car and crawled back the full distance on his elbows. he was an illustrator who lit up a book on fly fishing and a freelancer who produced architectural renderings so he could raise his family without the uncertainty of only being an artist. he was a romantic who loved his wife madly and who, deaf as a doorknob, had her hit a cowbell to get his attention. he didn't get along with my dad. they'd yell at each other on lakes, scaring the fish away. they'd yell about work. they'd yell about anything. Karl loved to paint. Dad hated the bank but did it for the dough and the phony prestige. he ragged on my uncle for not 'knowing the value of a buck' but Karl had the balls to be an artist and Dad wished he'd written books. Karl was a moralist who hated hearing that my dad cheated on my mom but who reversed himself when she divorced him—why couldn't she gut it out? back and forth they'd fume. it made my little boy head spin until i'd watch him paint, usually water colors propped up on easels in snow fields near our house in Connecticut. he'd work with quick, sure strokes, pipe in mouth, eyes squinting at a tobacco barn in the near distance. unlike my Dad, a word whore, Karl was a man who spoke with his eyes. one look from that mashed-in football face and i knew i'd found a grown-up who understood me, who recognized the artistic idiosyncrasies in my character and who sussed out a sensibility that few had guessed at (including me). he knew that i'd make unconventional choices as i sorted out wherever-the-fuck i was heading and was ok

with it. when we'd leave his house after a Thanksgiving/foot-
ball weekend, he'd nudge me aside and signal acknowledgment
with a wave of the pipe: a trail of smoke that let me know that
i'd be fine, no matter what, as if to tell me that the odd path
can be the right one, to listen to my heart, to keep at whatever
strange interest seduced me. sadly, after college, i saw little
of the man. i was caught-up chasing my whims all over the
game board—Peace Corps, architecture, teacher, hippie, actor.
none panned out until i began, unexpectedly, to write songs.
Karl heard about it. could i send him a tape? were the songs
honest? not sure his ears could hear, let alone judge what i sent
him, i felt a peculiar certainty knowing that my early work
mattered to him. then his kids grew up and scattered. he lost
his dear wife and began to lose touch with the real world. he
believed that credit cards were free money and he sand-castled
an Everest of debt. not able to hear, he mistrusted strangers
and became paranoid, fearful and accusatory. chronic vertigo tumbled him down stairs and he broke his ankle. he was
shuttled through hospital, rehab, a nursing home and assisted
living in a downward spiral that whirl-pooled him away from
his beloved self-sufficient life. the ankle wouldn't heal—the
doc cut bone from his hip to fix it—took a year and returned
him to the hateful nursing home. old ladies cackled about his
'hot legs' and winked. nurses made fun of him behind his back
and were inattentive. the medics messed him up. when he
got pneumonia, they doled out the wrong drugs. he became
delusional. he'd pop out of bed, wheeling his chair, spying and
making remarks with nobody paying attention. 'let's go for

a dip!' he'd shout. 'there's a pool upstairs and we gotta see Rick! he's up on the second floor, we gotta go see him. c'mon Karen (his daughter)!' she'd listen and shrug, teary-eyed, not knowing what to do, his life narrowing to nothing. his vertigo came back. he fell, broke his hip and was trapped again. it was hard for his kids to show up, their lives hurrying along with their own families to look after. he grew distant and dark and no one could find a solution. he didn't want anyone to save him. a blood clot in his heart (a pulmonary embolism) could have been averted had he been properly hydrated, but the docs failed again and he died. he must have hated this humiliating conclusion to a lion's life. he had become the dad his kids joked about, even as they loved him. as for me, i never went to visit. he died in that fucking rest home, bullshit about the last mile he could no longer crawl. my dad, like Hendrix, puked into his lungs on a Christmas Eve and choked to death, alone in a hospital in Boston with no kids, no wife, no girlfriend—nobody; a parallel to Karl's isolated demise. the brother's Kinscherf—a Russian novel from New Jersey.

CHRISTMAS ASH

stopped off at Waterman's Funeral Home around 6:30 to pick up Dad's remains. 'we've come to pick up some ashes.' 'yes. yes, of course. this way, please.' the man at the door greeted us with several expressions at once: condolence, pity, irritation, flatness. he told us to sit and wait in a paneled room. he came back with a box—a tan, cardboard box about six inches squared that had a sticker on it: the Forest Hills Crematory. Richard Gustave Kinscherf, Jr., 'Dad' in this pathetic box. it seemed ludicrous and cold. we drove back to his apartment on Mt. Vernon St. Dad inexplicably wanted his ashes scattered over Beacon Hill (he'd only lived here for two years). we took a bread knife from the kitchen and a single rose that someone had brought to the service earlier. Sam built a fire in the fireplace to burn the box after we finished upstairs. Lisa or Janie silently carried the thing and the serrated knife and we began the short climb to the roof. when we got to the top of the stairs and were about to open the door, a geezer in a bathrobe appeared in the hallway. 'hey! you can't go up there at night! it's not allowed! come down from there!' we stared down at him—Dad's children, weirded-out by this old Scrooge. 'i said come down from there. i got a wife sick in bed!' 'please, sir,' in my most controlled tone, 'there is something very important that we have to do and we are going to do it. no one is going to stop us. it won't be dangerous. we won't have to do anything like this again.' i don't mention the ashes. Scrooge retreated back into his apartment and slammed the door. it had been snowing all day, but had stopped to unveil a startlingly-clear night. snow crunched underfoot. Janie thought it'd be good to stand in a spot where the wind would catch the ashes and not blow them back into our faces. we approached the far end of the roof and peered down into the cobblestone alley below—it was deserted except for a Country Squire

station wagon. i bent down in the snow and began to cut open
the box. it was a struggle because it was tightly sealed and
had no mark on the outside to indicate which end was up. i
managed to crack into it, pieces of cardboard separating like
broken wings as Lisa and Janie held the flaps apart. inside
was a plastic bag filled with grey 'flakes': bits of bone and
wood and cavity fillings and unburnables—chips. as if Dad
had been shoved through a garbage disposal into a see-thru
burrito packet. we decided to hold on to the thing as three,
leaning out over the edge of the roof. we upended the bag
and a rush of the remains roared out of the box. they were
too heavy to float out over the city as Dad had imagined. we
were shocked and freaked as the inside plastic followed after:
a miniature parachute, partly-filled, chased after the debris
and landed with a smack on the windshield of the station
wagon below. straight down. no happy scattering whatsoever.
we were crying and laughing and pissed off that there was no
information about this sort of thing. couldn't this have been
a more graceful affair? we stumbled back into the apartment.
Sam's fire was roaring. we tossed the box into the flames. it
caught quickly and exploded back into the room—a fire spirit
straight out of The Lord of the Rings. we jumped. Sam picked
it up and shoved it back. we went downstairs to the street to
see what had happened. bits of Dad scattered all over the hood
and glass of the car. based on the license plate, 'Dad' would be
going to Rhode Island in the morning in a car he hated and a
state he had no liking for.

MA

Ma walks through fire, courageously it seems, without drawing attention to herself—alone except for a couple of friends
and her cat and her evening vodka tonics, independent of the
maelstrom of her long years with Dad and relatively independent of her bizarre children who seem to provide only
unusual, abnormal, odd problems: Rick's queer and unsuc-
cessful, Janie is a thoroughgoing Siddha who's 'worried about
having children because she wouldn't have enough time to
meditate (she got over that fast, thank God!)' and Lisa, who
finally slimmed down after blimping up, is getting a grip
on her own manic-depressive nature and sincerely loves and
gives to Ma ('she's too good to me'). so there she sits in her
gray-and-white, rather masculine and stylish, seersucker
bathrobe, newly purchased in Portland because 'sometimes
they wake you up in the middle of night to see the animals' on
her about-to-happen trip to Zanzibar. her white hair is fleecy
and shining after her short shower and she bends over the
Globe's crossword puzzle and the remains of her coffee, seem-
ingly at ease in these atypical homo-apartment surroundings.
we sit in silence, comfortably together after my twenty-four-
hour effort to keep her happy and proud of me, somehow, and
respectful, if not considerate, towards my boyfriend. i know
that i love her, i definitely do. she is not pathetic or blind and
even though she rarely volunteers her deeper feelings, i know
what they are. she loves all three of us completely, with nearly

unequivocal support and she chooses to never get in the way. i imagine her life to be solitary, even lonely, without sexual or emotional release, but she never complains if that is the case and appears to be sustained by some simple act of will, of Yankee self-ethic which tells her to be strong and fair and to help out where she can. she follows me in the MG (she bought a Horizon instead of a Rabbit because she wanted to be 'patriotic') to Brookline Village for gas and I send her on her way to New Haven. i don't remember telling her that i love her—i was in a hurry. i hope we won't run out of time. i hope i get rich quick in order to give her some financial security in her old age; i would hate to let her down. i hope we can have some longer space together some day, when she can lean on me for a change.

MY SISTER, LISA (RIDGEMONT ST, 1973)

i look at her and i forget she is my sister, or even someone i know. i am struck by how beautiful she is, of how impossible it is for her to pretend or perform herself. i wander about the house, lost to others, lost to myself and she sees and waits always for the right moment and says some small idea or suggestion or advice or wisdom or points out the humor in my blind-to-self-ness or brings me something to eat or drink and i am released or soon on the way to release from the grip of

some lethal obsession. i am in a state tonight because i seemed
to have lost a stupid demo cassette. i overturned every pouch
and pocket and shelf 20 times until i gave up, got mad—in
the grip of an hysterical faux-fever. Lisa, curled in the green
chair says, 'don't worry. go out. i'll find it. i have time.' with
magic, slow-motion deliberation, she begins probing with
her heavy hands—hands disproportionately out-sized—and
in minutes she finds the tape stuffed away in a box of my
envelopes. later, this note: Dear Rick, the thing i am going to
miss the most leaving the band (Orchestra Luna), is singing
your songs. although, while performing them, they seemed to
pass right through me. i love singing your songs. i can't listen
to, or enjoy, any other music as much. i realized this too late
that night Tommy played his tape for me—not the same. all i
felt was a desire to shut it off and play your stuff and become
excited and amused and nostalgic. but anyway, those tunes of
yours moved my heart, still move my heart. and that must be
why i stuck with it for so long. that's the truest thing about it
for me. i know that now. i wish i could put something in here,
into Dear Diary, so that when you opened the book you would
open to the most beautiful place in the world and we could all
just walk in. Lis

FIREWORKS

Dad said he had to talk to me. he was crying, his nose was red, he put his clumsy hand on my shoulder and said he wanted to read me a letter—a love letter from Molly. 'i love her. i love her. my God, i love her…Jesus Christ!' i hated her. he put his arms around me and squeezed me really hard and he kept on, sobbing. i didn't tell him that i hated her but his whole confession intruded heavily on my feelings for my Mom. i was only fourteen. weeks later, SP informed on him. it ruined their friendship. and when CK was visiting us, she and Ma walked off down the lawn, arm in arm. Ma was crying. Dad gave Molly up. or she gave him up. i can't remember. and there were others—college girls who 'understood.' it was a typical upbringing: a 50's family in a big house, lower-upper middle-class, private schools, summers at Prouts Neck, constant cocktails. but we were being exposed to some bizarre emotional fireworks. theirs was such a crazy chemistry, Mum and Dad. we had to believe they loved each other somehow. in some unseen way. all of this blew back later for us kids in ways visible and not. love lives of part-time uncertainty, self-doubt and fear of loss.

THE END IN SLOW MOTION

i was watching the tube and heard a crash and then a groan. i waited for the commercial and then walked out to the kitchen to check. Dad was on all fours, in his pajama top. his balls hung down like old tits, swaying from side to side. he was pushing a glass of vodka in front of him, first with the inside of his hand, then with the outside, like it was a hockey puck (one more 5th retrieved from the woodpile not discovered by my Mom and drained into the sink). 'you okay?' 'yeah, yeah, yeah.' he has a big dipper of strange red spots on his forehead. he's puking blood. he refuses to go to the hospital. he refuses to join AA or go to that ridiculous drying out center called Live-N-Grin (who can blame him?). he is using up the leftovers of his life fast, trying to make up for the extended stupor of his twenty-five-year-long marriage and job he hated at the bank. there's nothing any of us can do. that's what I tell myself. Lloyd claims that if you catch a guy by the hair as he's jumping off a cliff, okay but if he jumps again when your back is turned, it's none of your business. Dad definitely wants to jump. he's been jumping for years. a slow, pre-meditated, alcoholic suicide. i don't think the end is near, but it is coming. 'i'll predecease you,' he is forever promising Grandpa (the legal language of the estate planner). he cuts a big slobbering path through life—the old battle-ax thundering through the heat and the flies.

¶

EARLY WARNINGS

"I can quite truthfully say that I never lifted a hand unless for someone; never took up a brush or a pen, a sheet of music or a spade, never pursued a thought without the motivation of trying to make someone love me."
— *Sylvia Ashton-Warner*

HOT SPRINGS

it's 1968 and i'm eligible for a draft deferment if i teach school
or join the Peace Corps. terrified of Viet Nam, of killing or
being killed or of being a shitty teacher, i opt for the Peace
Corps (Korea) but get the boot halfway through training.
the shrink diagnoses me as a confrontational personality
that won't cut it in a non-confrontational society like Korea. i
would be the classic ugly American. my next try is for a teaching deferment. through Yale i land a job as a special class/
art teacher in a one-street town called Moosup (as in 'there's
a moose up the river'), Connecticut. i last eight months. i
fall in love with one of my students, E. he lives across the
street from my boarding house in a nearly-falling-into-the-
river, two-story shack with his mom, her boyfriend(s) and six
brothers and sisters. by winter, i am sleeping in his bed every
single night. no one minds. we are tentative, physically. i get
no sleep and tip-toe out in the morning, shoes dangling from
two fingers, rush across Main Street, dress for school and
get picked up by the football coach, heart in vertigo. Moosup
Junior High is not Eton or Exeter (where i imagine boys slept
with boys and/or teachers for centuries as a right of passage
and part of the curriculum). of course this is bullshit. i'm
working a public school in a tiny town with tiny minds. E will
be found out, shamed or worse. god knows what might happen
to me. i decide the best thing for everyone is to skip town.
i ride to Philly on my Kawasaki 650, depressed and weakly

suicidal. when i call E up, 20 years later, his son answers:
'Dad's out,' he says. i tell him who i am, how i knew his dad
and before i can finish explaining the kid shouts, 'Rick!? from
Moosup?!' like i'm some long lost hero, back from traversing
the globe, the person his father told him about. when E takes
the phone, he tells me that i wouldn't like him now. that he
has a pot belly and isn't 'that way' anymore. he says we'd been
good with each other then and still are today. maybe we'll
get a beer if he comes up north. this conversation occurs long
after i try, one short year after Moosup, to take a second crack
at teaching. this time in a co-ed boarding school in Steamboat Springs, Colorado. what was i thinking? sure enough,
three months down the road i have 'those feelings' again,
this time for K, my english student. we spend hours together,
get wrecked on Robitussin and take long walks in the snow,
the electricity of high emotion and laughter bouncing off the
hills. sometimes i lie in his lower bunk, he in the upper we
hold hands top to bottom, not saying a word, smiling. we
drive to the top of a hill, take off our clothes and slip into the
hot springs, floating there, at peace and forgetting school,
job, drama, age difference (i am 21, he's 16) and thrive in the
moment, close, a bit in love. it is a rare, psychedelic oasis on
top of a Colorado peak and though we never 'do anything,'
i'm 'caught,' accused of sleeping with boys AND girls and
fired. they shunt me off to a motel where i drop acid and wait
until one of my teacher friends sneaks K down to see me one
last time. we hold each other, cry some and then, next day, he
goes back to school and i take the bus to Denver for my draft

physical, acid high and scared to death. i flunk. i have letters from two shrinks that are conclusive: i am both 'suicidal AND homicidal,' a 4F. this was the ignominious end to both my last stand as a teacher and dodging bullets in Nam. i write K long letters about everything, missing him. i guess they were love letters. the headmaster reads them aloud to the student body at lunch in the cafeteria embarrassing my friend and doom- ing our relationship. i try to repair the damage by driving to Santa Barbara and waiting for him when he flies home for Christmas. but when he arrives he doesn't want to see me. it had been too much to bear, the public humiliation. it is a long, amphetamine-fueled drive home. i suppose even as i was terrified and partly ashamed of everything that went down, it was time to take seriously the idea that i might become that infamous identity: artist/musician/homo.

PROM DATE

i was in charge of both of them, junior and senior. how did that happen? did i have an inkling (or did my classmates) that i was, you know, 'good that way'? i had skills: decorating, organizing, stage directing, delegating, making something pretty out of ugly. junior year we took over a former chapel and erected scrims, backlit with life-size cut-out silhouettes of speakeasy figures playing horns and dancing, high and happy. we transformed an unappealing rectangle into teen

noir. i asked a girl from summer vacation to come down
from Boston to Philly for the big night. i knew she was not a
going-out-with girl, but someone who would make me look
cool on the twist-again-like-we-did-last-summer dance floor
and who was terrifically cute, with a wispy Mia Farrow voice.
maybe i hoped she'd make it seem as if i 'scored.' at any rate
the effort got me elected class-fucking-president and senior
prom chairlady. over the summer before our last shot at living
at home and breaking all the rules, my best friends and i got
drunk on a beach in Avalon, NJ. cold beer was delivered (we
ordered by phone with our 'Dad' self). crushed cans littered
the sidewalk from porch to ocean. throughout, i was thinking (God help me) 'prom.' when we spotted a 50's cover band
loading into a VFW hall, we got their card and booked them,
puffed up about what a hot ticket we knew they'd be. live
music was a rarity in those days. standing next to a bonfire
and staring at the stars we decided that for this last-in-a-life-
time promenade we would transform the high school gym, a
big, nasty, echoing, sweaty box, into an out-of-the-park-into-
the-gym garden. we'd 'appropriate' trees, flowers, shrubbery,
earth, rocks, worms and weeds as a full-on midnight caper.
we got a van and a pick up truck. we blackened our faces
like teen-age special forces. we appropriated our weapons
of choice—hedge clippers, saws, gloves and goggles—as we
cruised the hood and stole Eden. motoring up to the shoulder of a Main Line mansion, we'd belly crawl to an innocent
tree or bush, hack at it and watch it quiver, seize up, tip over
and collapse—a green corpse dragged across an immaculate

lawn and flipped into the van. we did this over and over again until we had enough garden poofery to convert the gym into 'paradise.' it even smelled like outdoors. 'how did you guys pull this off?' the faculty advisor asks. 'we ah...i dunno...we just did it. contributions from families of the class of '63.' i asked another summertime girl to be my 'date,' girl as corsage. she looked like Natalie Wood in Rebel Without a Cause—a total babe. god knows i must have disappointed her in the get-it-on department, but so what. my huge, over-compensatory event made the girlfriend ruse worth the ticket and besides, i loved impersonating an impresario. i suppose it carried over into all that show-biz fluff i did later on. funny about high school.

ALPHA BEFORE OMEGA

the homo recog: when did it happen? when did i know for sure that it wasn't going to be Geigering girls? i remember feeling all sorts of something for Stevie lying face down on the floor of his well-worn living room rug reading comics leg to leg but it wasn't anything that stuck in my seven-year-old brain. playing Flash Gordon in a barn, we de-pantsed each other one smokey afternoon but no 'hey, faggot' light bulb popped on. Richard (the new kid in second grade) and i told each other that boys were better than girls 'all over' and were 'comparing' on my bed when my grannny burst into the room and yelled at us for 'being bad,' her face angry-cop red. we

didn't get it. we weren't sure what she was riled up about. we
certainly weren't aware that our identity was anything out
of the ordinary. next up: the canvas covered haystack probe.
Brandy called them 'boner cosmetics.' he persuaded the boys
across the street and me to take off our blue jeans so he could
nudge a carefully whittled and greased 'dick stick' into our
tiny, reluctant pink entryways. not so far as to hurt or suggest
anything 'weird' but just because. to tell the truth we liked
to watch and it felt sorta ok but still, when it all went down,
there was no queer alarm. i can mentally Polaroid the boy
who came over to our house with his family to let us pick out
a Basset Hound puppy. he stood on a stone wall above me and
i could see up his too short frenchie shorts, no underwear. his
tiny testicles hung like apricot pits in crinkly skin. it kind of
excited me but i didn't know why. i shrugged it off. i felt up
and got felt up by Gib when his family came to town—crayon
erections under damp sheets. but that was just something we
did when he came over. didn't everybody? i still had miles to
go before i got it about being bent. i slept over John's house
in a bed too small for two. he'd reach down below and touch
me up until i got a stiffy and had to go to the bathroom.
something other than piss came out. it looked like puss and
frightened the shit outta me. i thought i'd caught a disease but
i kept it to myself. you can't talk about dick when you're nine,
not with clarity or safety or cool and definitely not in 1954.
i was sure it would be girls in my future anyhow, that's how
it was supposed to be, until Kin broke down all the barriers.
he'd asked me to lie on top of his back with my gear in his

ass crack and that's when it happened, that's when the white
stuff did a spit shot in my underwear. i was 13, a late bloomer,
but that's when it clicked. that's when i wanted to do it again.
to set it up. to revisit the 'moment.' to give him a woody and
make cum come out of him. but Kin was oddly unavailable
after our bedroom camp-out and there were no more sleep-
overs. plus i'd been warned: a friend insinuated, 'be careful.
Kin and his brothers do things, dirty things at night.' so i
kept my distance even though this piece of news made the
possibility of a re-enactment all the more exciting. i waited in
the wings and it wasn't til i was 16, be-zitted and able to drive
that i took matters in hand. one morning around three a.m.,
i drove to Kin's house, tip-toed up to his room on squeaky
stairs and climbed into his bed. i wanted to get him off the
way he got me off but he acted strangely, ornery and horny at
the same time. when i felt him up (pistol hard), he rolled to
the far side of the bed and made conflicting sounds: back-of-
the-throat gasps versus sneering disgust. had he uncovered
homo files on himself that he wanted to reject? was he as
uncomfortable and freaked out as i had been months before?
i slid out from under the covers, boner bobbing, and headed
home. part-way down the stairs he called out in a whisper
for me to come back. that it was ok. that he was ok. that i
could, i should, you know... but i was too wigged out. i left
and that was that. no more Kin. no more foolin' around. i was
not gonna be a homo, no sir. i was going to fight back in my
solitary teen tower until i wanted girls the way i wanted him.
i slipped up here and there with an occasional 'we're not actu-

ally doing what were doing while we're doing it' encounters.
there was the rip-off-the-towel wrestling match with Billteam
captain, in a swimming pool cabana. ok, we weren't wrestling.
flagpole erections quivered in the dank and the dust, but we
never talked about it. i stuffed all erotic tug-of-wars deep in
my psyche until i graduated from college and became, as a
teacher, intimately involved with one of my students. he lived
across the street from my boarding house. love, sex and the
promise of scandal converged to bring me out of the closet.
meanwhile, i heard that: 1) good ol' Kin had tried to schuss
down Mt Washington (the speed record for downhill still
stands on that mountain). he fell near the top and broke all
four limbs, and 2) charging down a motel hallway chased by
horny brothers, he bolted through a plate glass window and
cut himself to pieces. this kid, who is most likely married with
children and grandchildren by now, brought it out of me, so
to speak, a predilection that was inevitable, irrevocable and
ultimately beautiful. i think about him often. i recapture those
first, awkward, stinky steps. i owe him a nod for facing myself
and my true truth.

C R Y

he led the choir, glee club and the middle school chorus where
i went to school (the Episcopal Academy in Philly). he taught
music appreciation and coached softball. his initials, C. R. Y.,

proved to be an acronym that spelled it out—his passion and his unfair downfall in my eyes. when i was 12 i auditioned for choir/chorus. i was terrified as i stood next to him at the piano: he played scales, i sang them back, the notes resonating in my small bird's chest like a miniature Tibetan bell. the thrill of this new thing, this singing in a girl's soprano, ran from my heels up my spine to the crown of my head. it wasn't really a girl's soprano, it was a boy's. there is a subtle difference. the sound is as pure as silver ringing out of little mouths, little 'o's' on the upturned faces of cherubs. we never, at least not at our school, thought this was sissy. it was instead a huge credit to be singing in the choir, chorus (soprano/alto) and later the glee club. it probably got me into Yale with its diehard singing group tradition. i loved it so much, lost in a sea of voices at the spring concert (recorded on swimming-pool blue vinyl), filing past him to see if he'd give a meaningful wink. we felt special. we really truly did. to be awarded a solo was the pinnacle of the rush—a single, fluted voice rising above 120 others to dove-soar across the gymnasium and land in the hearts of adoring, astonished friends and parents. certainly my infatuation and eventual life obsession with music and singing began here, with Mr. CRY. as seniors we took his music appreciation class and covered the symphonic and opera classics with gusto. his enthusiasm was contagious and real. at the end of the school year he'd take us to his favorite Italian restaurant in downtown Philly where waiters sang opera and where we had our first inkling of a non-family dinner out with wine, song and romantic escapade.

he was short and had a pencil mustache and up-combed, wavy, ink-black hair. we worshipped him. we sought his approval. after i went off to Yale and ultimately became a Whiffenpoof (even recording in the big room at the Columbia Studios in Manhattan) i wanted to give him the result. i was proud of it. i thought he would be as well, especially my big gutsy version of 'Sit Down You're Rockin' The Boat.' i called him up and he asked me to meet him as his apartment. sure, i thought. sounds good. i was, at the time, in the (cluttered) closet. i'd been found out at Yale by others like myself, but none of them attracted me and to those who knew, i swore i'd 'fix' myself. meanwhile i was falling in mad love with the less sure and doing nothing about it in bed. at Episcopal we had, as kids, theories about some of the teachers. who 'was' and who 'wasn't.' somehow Mr. CRY. never made the list. i guess we loved him too much to stain our sense of who he was with nasty schoolboy gossip. so it was with a naïve heart that i drove to his place to see him, catch up, maybe have a more open conversation about art or something and of course, to play the Whiff record. when i got there he'd already had a few and was red in the face, even a bit weepy. i knew it like a gun went off that Mr. York was gay as a goose and damned if i was gonna tell him i was too. he seemed to like the record enough, but it was me, grown up, now 21, that he wanted to see, to talk with, as if he could come clean about all the boys over the years that he'd loved and never had. how his heart must have hurt to suppress those feelings. we'd heard that he took vacations to the west coast. maybe it was there that he acted out, maybe not. at any rate i wanted outta there. he came forward to hug me. i guess i hugged him back like a whore worried about her hair or about touching too close down there. it was brief, awkward and sad. this man, this wonderful man who had brought so much to so many had had to hide all those years. hide from the scorn that would have inevitably chewed him alive. hide from the feelings he had for those up-chinned boy sopranos. hide, hide, hide. it tears me up to think about him, even though i know i could never have been even remotely his friend. i guess love requires illusion. C. R. Y. created one of the most beautiful i have ever known.

¶

APPEARANCE

"Either that wallpaper goes, or I do."
— *Oscar Wilde*

CLOTHES HORSE

i am not turned out. i never give it a thought. i tell myself i'm
ok with it. i can pass as someone who dresses adequately. it's
the same today as it was when i was a kid. in high school i
wore the standard blazers and sweaters, nothing exceptional.
i looked all right leaving the house, but as soon as i got to
school i was a disaster—cereal on tie, milk on pants, loafers
crushed at the heel, shirt tail out, dandruff on shoulders and
ink stains on shirt cuffs. today, the last place i spend cash is on
clothes. i shop Old Navy, The Salvation Army and Boomer-
angs. i buy dumb t-shirts and generic pants with too many
pockets. the t's have armpit holes, dated logos and they're
getting bigger—Hawaiian mumu. from XL to XXXL they've
become the Super Bowl of t's. they tent over my beer belly
like a deflated all weather dome. sometimes i experiment with
color. red t, green pants—Christmas-y. brown on brown—
Miles Davis-y. black-on-black—DKNY-sy. i make no dent in
hipster-ville. as for the shoes? my party shoes? buxom Doc
Martin boots, scuffed up like scabs and worn rarely. the laces
are ravaged and stressed out like raw nerves. they require
'orthotics'—layered strips of rubber that lift and twist my
right heel to make one leg longer or shorter than the other
and to take the pressure off my hip and lower back. my podiatrist intones, "forget surgery; go with the orthotics" (which is
hard to pronounce without a lisp...orthotixth). they slide like
stubborn trout into the bottoms of my 'beasts,' the sneakers

he also insisted upon, which at $120 a pop, are as expensive as they are ugly. they come in bleach-white only, like nurse's marshmallow shoes and are, within a week, transformed into petri dishes of Doyle's drippings and droppings, the white smudged out, my big toenail poking through the upper front and busting a peek-hole that looks like an inflamed asshole. maybe they should call them that: 'assholes.' anyhow, i wear these more than the party boots just because i don't want to bother with the trout transfer and i figure who's gonna look at my feet anyway? perhaps if i had short people 'lifts' or cha-cha heels i'd seem more in style, but i gave that up years ago. like Popeye says: 'i yam what i yam'—a pig in a t-shirt with fat shoes.

MY RIDICULOUS HAIR

i'm not sure if there was ever a time in my life when my hair was anything but ridiculous. whether from my point of view or from others, on stage or off, or in that netherworld where the two get mixed up. maybe, when i was a boy with a wiffle, it was ok. in the family scrapbook i look 'regular'—buzzed, traditional and predictable from the end of high school through Yale, the song remaining the same—short all over, wisp flip above forehead and fat face. this was followed by the acid years: carefree undulating slippery hippie Jesus hair. in my LSD trip to the mirror i looked almost cool, a dude, under a Gandalf wide-brim, hanging in soft Shirley Temple clumps that came alive like Medusa snakes. i added an under-beard and looked Amish. in my passport photo i resembled a dagger-eyed Rasputin. it turns out that facial hair is as much trouble as head hair. i can't grow sideburns. they stop a quarter inch below the spot where they are supposed to weave in with the 'hair' hair. my soul patch is a Triscuit—a sad, off-yellow piece of punctuation that takes weeks to become noticeable. i tell my friend Ben there's a long list of people who don't like it. 'add me to the list,' he says. that's the other part of the problem—other people. they hate whatever 'do i do. i say fuckit. buzz the shit off. go for Dachau. get a cinchy no-haircut haircut. what the Doyle's girls go for. 'makes you look younger, Ricky,' they say. which is absurd. nothing can make you look younger. it's like a facelift. the neck crêpe is a dead giveaway. next up: dye jobs. i tried them all—ugly black, peroxide green-blonde, Irish Setter red. my favorite was Mallard duck: a dark, neon blue/green. 'honey,' squeals my poofter hair dresser, 'you will look FABulous!' hours-in-the-chair-and-under-the-dryer later my 'do has become a diaph-anous swimming-pool blue. i race home, squirt CVS product all over myself to repair the damage only to make it worse—a drab Buster Brown. going in another direction, i attempt a do-it-yourself cellophane—a translucent iodine-do that, at a visit to a local swimming hole populated by African Ameri-cans, the colored girls dug: 'dat color is da shit, girl! how you do dat?' no one else agrees. in fact, traveling to Prague i real-ize that all the ex-commie old ladies have the same cellophane

job i had and it looks like the color of a nuclear sun. in the
meantime, the haircuts get wilder. i shave the sides, frou-frou
a limp rooster tail on top, try braids, bangs and perms. where
am i? who am i? is there any hope? lately, i just let it grow—
long, tired and seaweed stringy. in the morning i am Neil
Young on a bender dancing with a bag lady. at night i slop
on a glue-like Hispanic gel, smear it hard-as-glass and hope
for Pat Riley but wind up with Planet of the Apes or worse: a
sociopathic sex offender. 'when are you going to cut it, Rick?
it's really ugly and it makes you look old.' at this point i don't
give a fuck. i like that it's odd. i'm odd. Berlin as a b-movie
rubber monster.

FAT FACE

every single morning, out of the sack i fart, piss, feed my
cat, rip open the curtains, choke down vitamins and park in
front of a computer. every single morning. but today i notice a
strange hot tingling expanding on surface of my chest. it ekes
its way up my neck, down across my forearms, onto my face
and then, as if sunburned from the inside out, the skin on my
cheeks begins to bloat as if Botox is being injected into all the
wrong places. instead of ironing out a crevasse, it plumps up
the skin on either side creating an aerial Grand Canyon of my
face. i look as grotesque and distorted as the Elephant Man.
in the mirror i see the distortion with horror-movie horror

(hands on the side of my face and a silent scream). after 30, 40 minutes, it goes away. my doc thinks it's a late-developing allergic reaction to the vitamin ammo i've been shoving down my throat for the last 30 years. i'm gonna try not taking them and keeping an eye peeled. should it happen again, i'll take a sped-up, time-lapse video—a narcissist's nightmare on Centre Street.

FISHNETS

you make a snap decision and it turns out to be a fiasco. this time it was fishnets: lime-green, sparkly fishnets. i try them on at a college gig—a fucking college. i'm wearing short shorts, a see-thru skimpy ladies 'blouse,' gold, reflective Converse All Stars and fucking lime-green fishnets. if this was a nod to glam, to Bowie, to some consistent 'look,' maybe i could have cut it. but no, this was a fluke. it came out of left field. it was right up there with the gold lamé pajamas i wore for an Orchestra Luna show at the Orpheum. the band didn't get written up, but the pajamas did. 'jumping around the stage like a hot potato in tin foil.' good going, Berlin. but still, on the top of the embarrassment mountain were the lime-green fishnets with my leg hair squirting out between the gnarly threads.

FANTASY NAILS

a few birthdays back i decided to creep up on (i didn't want
to get caught with my feet in a swirl bucket by unsuspecting
friends) Fantasy Nails—the Korean manicure shop on Centre
St. —for a pedicure from the ferocious lady, a tiny broad who
yanked one foot out of the swirl bucket and went at my toenails with a pair of cutter teeth that looked like stainless-steel
choppers on a psycho beaver. i stared at Japanese rock videos
on a silent screen as my feet shriveled in the swirl. to be honest, i was glad to get the lady. the guy was too delicate (a subtle application of eye liner). i wanted tough love from the bitch
on my gnarled, dog-hard toenails which had become warped
gruesome-ugly because, as a killer nun in Jim Steinman's
never-to-be-fully-mounted musical Neverland, i leaped from
the stage, landed on an electric cable and broke my foot. you
don't get a cast for that sort of injury, you hobble and wait
and in the end your foot is a disaster. you know that photo of
Baryshnikov's feet? how they looked after decades of being
crushed en pointe? they were like that. my big right toe is
twisted and bent and my toenails look like fungus muffins.
which is why i treated my birthday-self to Fantasy Nails in
the first place. i wanted a makeover. pulling one heel out
of the water, dagger-eyes swiped a cheese slicer across the
bottom of my foot and scraped centuries of yellow callous
away into the bubbly in larded lumps. the bottoms of my feet
were now soft as a puppy's belly. still, i'm nervous. i remember Polanski's Repulsion. Catherine Deneuve as a manicurist

snipped a vein as she pared the cuticles of an elderly man. black blood squirted over white linen and soundless screams ricocheted off the walls (my fantasy at Fantasy Nails became a nightmare). about a year after the procedure an arsonist torched the place and now Fantasy Nails is kaput. i tried alternatives. none have made the grade. who's gonna make my feet once-a-year-new now? me. privatization. when my roommates are out of the apartment i fill a spaghetti pot with hot water, soak and chop at my screwed-up nails, one foot hiked on the tub, my ass on toilet and my cat meowing outside the door. with the soak pot replacing the hi-end swirl, i'm able to snip my softened nails and nibble off the weird, Stonehenge shapes with impunity. i feel naughty and in-a-hurry fearful of the unexpected roommate catching me in the act. like Mom barging into a teenage bedroom at the 'wrong time.'

GOLF TITS

i see them; those bright-shirted, middle-aged men (Tiger, too) lumbering down the links in the blazing sun. there they jiggle: the dude boobs. left, right, up, down, shiver and shake—they make me laugh. i wonder if the wives in their lives look over at the tube while spooning slobber up baby's chin and notice them, their husband's titties and think: 'how did he let this happen?!' i don't play the game, but i sport my own omelette-y pair. i sense them bobbing about in my t-shirt

as i careen around Doyle's. there they are in the window.
there they are in the mirror. there they are when i bend over
to take an order. do they cleave? should one have work done?
do the lovers in our lives go for them? are they something
to squeeze, to feel comfy with as the waist expands? on the
mountain top of the male rack, the prime example are golf-
ers' titties. it doesn't make sense. they're athletes, right? they
walk around a lot. some slave carries the bag, but the players
tromp up and down the fairways and soldier on. do they scarf
down pizza and beer between strokes? do they huff or puff off
camera? do they encourage their titties as a counter balance
to an effective swing? would a sports bra squeeze them flat
and sweaty? do they hurt? will they require a mastectomy at
the 19th hole? do they even care that they have Jello boobs
dancing like miniature fat girls in their Nike shirts? has vanity yet to strike the greens? i think about guitar hero pecs—
those perky pikers above heroin-lean abs. those guys look
good. they don't play golf. ah ha! so, that's it—the game itself!
slapping testicular globs across OCD lawns, have they been
unconsciously castrating themselves into chicks with dicks?

FRONT/SIDE

you see a face from the side, the profile and the person is a
total knock-out until he turns and everything looks different.
his face is too wide, eyes are too small and his lower lip looks

weird. and it's the same in reverse. from the front, he's scary
handsome and then he turns and he's a chinless wonder with a
shark-fin nose. of course if we like them, they become beautiful, they 'are' beautiful. if we get bored, whatever they had in
beauty stock gets deleted, attraction being the great deceiver,
because for most of us, classic beauty is like classic rock on
classic radio—a milkshake that tastes great at first and later
makes you nauseated. and then there's our very own face.
we know it too well and not at all. on acid we're a Picasso,
cracked across the bridge of the nose, infinitely sad and funny
all at once. it's not unlike hearing our voice recorded and
played back for the first time. THAT'S me!? that grotesque,
narrow-nasal embarrassing sound which can never be gotten
used to? others know that voice and face and to them it's who
you are, how you look, what you sound like. all these are parts
of the ever-impossible-to-put-together-and-make-sense-of—
the depth of surface.

BACK OF HAND

Sorella's—regular Sunday breakfast and book. i spray
anti-melanoma, level-100 sunblock over exposed skin, glasses
hooked on nose to be able to read menu and book. i telescope
in on the back of my meaty truck driver's hand, my right
hand. the spray block has made the skin reflective and shiny
as if polyurethaned and preserved like an outdoor deck: piss

on it and you won't make a dent. or like the burnt skin of a
roasted turkey. neither metaphor pleases until i realize i am
seeing my mother's hand, the back of her hand, veined like a
trellis, spotted with freckles and asymmetrical brown shapes
of varying size. one in particular resembles Rhode Island, a
state that means nothing to me, but there it is, in miniature
on the back of my 70-year-old paw. as my train chases the
'golden year' goal posts i laugh at myself and wonder how i
will deal with the end of life—a map of which i can see, like
a pirate's treasure, on my bewildered hand—gracefully or
curmudgeonly threatening with a cane.

¶

MUSIC

"There is a vitality, a life force, an energy, a quickening that is translated through you into action, and because there is only one of you in all time, this expression is unique. And if you block it, it will never exist through any other medium and will be lost."
— Martha Graham

"There is a song walking down the street everyday and if you don't go out and shake its hand, someone else will."
— Nick Cave

YELLOW TEETH

i got a baby grand from my parents when i turned nine; big
and black and calling out to me like a harpie on a crag: 'try
me if ya can, kid but watch out, i'm a tough motherfucker.' it
was shiny and seemed to ask too much—all those 88's extend-
ing from one horizon to another. made me nervous. i stayed
near the center, near middle C. the sound of a single note, held
down and reverberating sang in my chest like a money shot
(the one i was yet to have). driven to lessons by my stubborn
sneak-a-shot-o'-likker granny in her dark blue Ford, a line
of honking cars stretched out behind us on the mountain
road, 'fuck 'em' in her set jaw. i trembled. i hated those lessons. i hated the music paper. i fogged out on the precisely
inked notes. my struggle to transmit them to fingers made
no sense. at my first recital, a child's song, i froze. i ran out
the door, fighting tears. months later i returned to the beast
and experimented with the dark, tentative notes resounding
from the hulking walrus, amounting to zip but mesmerizing
my pre-teen brain. down the road i improvised an 'original
composition' at a talent show at Prout's Neck, our summer
vacation spot in Maine. got a big ovation. i was 14, showing
off my Twist-N-Shout moves on the dance floor and covered
with zits. i compared thigh muscles with a kid from Rhode
Island. 'boys are better,' he said. i was silent, but i remembered
him as a part of that summer when i made friends with the
piano. after we moved to Philly we gave the lessons another
try. this time with some quack-invented system to fire up a

left hand accompaniment to whatever horrible pop song was
on the radio. it launched me once more into the refusenik
orbit. 'all you need is a melody,' he promised. you are so full
of shit, i thought. i quit two weeks in. meanwhile, across the
street in Wayne, procrastinating homework, our friends the
V's and a future Oberlin organ student, Henry and i played
'guess who this is?'—a crush clue on the keys that was supposed to identify someone we all knew—an early warning
of what eventually became song 'portraiture'—the wordless
snapshot. the summer of my last year in high school i was a
counselor at Camp Munsee, in the Poconos. in a barn slept a
lonely, scabby, out-of-tune upright. after the boys were asleep
i snuck down and played and was transfixed. not by anything
i was doing but by the sound, the awesome celestial echo. the
notes bouncing off pin-point stars. at Yale, same thing but
with drugs. in a college tower, i locked the door, dropped acid,
played with eyes shut and hallucinated psychedelic film clips
as they un-spooled, fingers hammering with faux-Stravinsky
cluster up and down the nicotine ivories. i kept it on the down
low. it was awful, i'm sure, but i kept going back, transported
by the thrill of this surging Hudson River of sound. two
years later, back in New Haven, living in a house full of nutty
artists and musicians, i cranked the motor up all over again.
we snatched an upright from a church and for the first time,
inspired by musician friends Francesca and Ed, i began to
crunch improvisations into songs like a blind man in a junk
store, just trying to tell the truth and to hit my compatriots in
the heart. maybe it never gets better than that. maybe it gets
worse.

VOX HUMANA

the singing began in Tuscon, leaning over an Andrews Sisters
78 rpm of 'Shrimp Boats Is A Comin.' i was mesmerized. i
gazed at the round-n-round trying to sing along in a boy-
as-chipmonk squeak. it was not until entering middle school
at the Episcopal Academy that i 'got' the transcendental side
of singing. C.R.Y. was our music teacher, chorus/glee club
conductor and choir master. i was 11. my voice had that pure,
no-vibrato soprano that we were led to believe was ok (not
girly). Mr. CRY, after all, coached baseball. we auditioned
(200 cherubs) with dime-sized mouths and tiny lifted chins. if
we did well, we made choir. we sight read, without knowing
the notes. the dots went up and down. it wasn't that hard. if
we were 'gifted' we earned a solo spot in that swath of boys
at the annual concert. the sensation of 200 voices, rising
from rib cages strong and clear and into the gymnasium air,
was my true introduction to music, physical, emotional and
spiritual. i remember wanting to sit next to whomever was
my pre-homo 'best friend' at the time. i'm pretty sure that
all that singing was a major part of what got me into Yale
where there is a huge singing tradition. glee, choir and all
those gentlemen songsters led triumphantly up the Whiffenpoof Alps (seniors only) who in tight ('tight') formation
cast their anachronistic spell. the arrangements, some by
Cole Porter (a grad), were stunning, complex and irresistible. i wasn't sure how i fit in with those guys socially. most

of them were high-powered preppies and had that haughty,
upper-class thing down to a white-shoe-T. i was locked in the
closet and terrified. still, the music was worth the discom-
fort. i loved being surrounded by that thick vocal river. we
drank and sang, wore white tie and tails and tilted slightly
forward off-heel as if to put a careful nose on the perfect note.
down the road, when i began to write my own songs, i hit a
wall, a vocal wall. i brayed and squawked and fought to hear
a voice that fit in with pop or rock, but what i heard bouncing back from the studio monitors sounded like an operatic
Whiffenpoof, or worse, a Broadway-chorus-boy nasal tenor.
i was appalled. i went to great lengths to make it sound 'rock
right,' ultimately damaging my vocal chords and necessitat-
ing two polyp operations. the first E.N.T. doc warned that a)
i would never sing again or b) would sound like Doris 'Que
Sera, Sera' Day (which, when i think about it, might not have
been such a bad idea). i got myself a second opinion, had the
things scraped off and resumed my band obsession. when my
boyfriend joined up, possessing a voice closer to Paul Rogers
than Ethel Merman, i was asking for it: 'why doesn't HE sing
all the songs? his voice is WAY more commercial.' my band
mates whined, 'we're treading industry water here with your
weird voice.' there was even a vote to throw me out of my own
band and have the, now ex-, boyfriend do all the singing. it
wasn't until i got back to playing my songs on the piano and
using my whatever-it-sounded-like voice honestly and not
trying to parody some asshole rock slut, that i came into my
own. singers can be the most neurotic of performers. on a loud

stage they can't even hear themselves think. to lose your voice in that environment is a nightmare. it's all you have. you can't turn it up to ten. what to do? NO MORE BANDS. as a solo dude i finally sound like me. i love it all over again as if, chin tilted upward, i'm in that miraculous innocent winged orbit of the boy soprano, eyes crossed, floating towards the stars.

BAND PARENTS

are not the same as stage moms or hockey dads. they don't show up during childhood. it's not until the kids are in college and have left the nest. then it begins, the nightmare. i watch them having dinner with their son before a gig at a nearby club. they look lost, anxious and dispirited. they make innoc-uous conversation in hopes of Windex-ing the glass on their blurry imaginings: 'seems like a nice enough club, dear, but it's so...dirty;' 'how do you get people to actually show up for these things? it must be awfully hard;' 'i can't hear the words and you wrote 'em, right? don't you think they're important?' anticipating the D-Day of distortion: 'we shoulda have picked up some earplugs, honey, doncha think?' later, inside the club: 'god, we look old, stand-out old. all these idiots bobbing their heads like dolls to whatever it is the music is saying to them and whatever it is that it's saying we don't get;' 'he sure seems to drink a lot on stage;' 'the owner's a prick, a loud mouth prick;' 'that fat girl looks ridiculous in a mini skirt;' 'why

does he close his eyes when he's singing?;' 'why does he say
'fuck' so much on the microphone?;' 'he loves what he's doing
i suppose but his drummer's a real asshole;' i can't wait to get
outta this coke hole.' they notice their own graying hair, bald
spots, pot bellies and motherly skirts and yet they put up with
it. they put up with him. they're not sure why. they don't talk
to each other at the club. all the drinks in the world make no
dent in their demeanor. meanwhile, under the table, they pray
that this is a phase he'll grow out of. they realize that 'fall
back on' is a pipe dream for their ever practicing son who,
holed up in his bedroom all through high school, zits galore,
shredding guitar and straining to zap out a zillion notes in
front of the mirror is in this for the long run. they worry
that maybe he'll fall through a crack they can't see coming.
they worry he'll catch some fatal S.T.D. they worry that the
void between what their kid is doing and their own world is
unbreachable. they listen as carefully as they can to the demo
they had to pay for and begin talking above the music long
before the first song is over, unable to pay attention let alone
comprehend what they hear. unexpectedly, Dad gets weepy.
for some reason art and sound moves him in spite of himself, a catch-in-the-throat pride in his black sheep son. had
he become a heroin addict or a transexual, things could have
been worse, though maybe more manageable than having to
support his stupid band at ugly clubs where woo-hoo's and
tennis claps add up to zilch. where loading in and loading out
seems endlessly tiresome. where the money is non-existent.
they don't get it and hate not getting it and wish they didn't

have to try. you feel badly for them even though you can't extend a hand. they do look silly and sad. they don't know their kid anymore. Santa Claus is long gone and their boy's dream impossible to imagine, let alone believe in or want for him. will his kids be stock brokers? they can only hope.

WHY DON'T I KNOW THE SONG?

'Rick, that song on the radio, what is it?' 'what song? i can't hear it. (tinitis, first off and if i could, i wouldn't know what it is anyhow). the real problem: i know next to nothing about about the history of music. big-time songwriters ladder-up the Bunyan shoulders of beloved predecessors, right? you can tell from the interviews. 'oh, yeah. when i heard _____ for the first time, i knew, deep down, that i had to _____ so they listened. they got it. they danced on the hum wire of the artist-to-artist umbilical chord, birth by proxy. when a 'new' song shivered out of them it was often a tip-of-the-hat to bygone music warriors. when something familiar reaches my ears i recall neither the name of the tune nor the artist or worse, the wrong name and the wrong artist. i stroke my chin as i watch earnest fans bump, grind and sing, word/ melody perfect, along with the tunes blasting in a bar or on the radio or in ear buds and i'm flabbergasted. how do they know this shit? as if they ARE the song, reliving the exact time and place when it first hit their hearts, replaying the timeless camaraderie of 'hey, we were there, you 'n me babe, right? remember?' the smarm that creams over the tune choices for weddings, start-up relationships and the death of loved ones. but for me it's a wash. i can't make out the words for the life of me. i wish i could, i do but tinitis combined with the study task it would take to educate myself would turn it into a homework assignment. listen to the tune, absorb it, master it, memorize it. i don't. i can't. i like to hear from someone else about a song. about how it was recorded, why it was written and why it holds meaning for my friend. but that's the end of it. it is my beer allies, my co-wokers or even total strangers that compel me to write music. it's their stories, failures, troubles and love-labors lost that appeal to my vampiric stenographer. it's them, my pals, not the famous, that get me. and also movies as shortcuts to actual life. Be Here to Love Me (the doc about Townes Van Zandt) became the inspiration for a tune i dedicate to him even as i know next to nothing about his music or lyrics. and another thing? i 'see' picture-scapes when i write, soundtrack hallucinations (it's always been like that, starting in college when i dropped acid, locked myself in a tower with an upright, closed my eyes and improvised whatever cerebral celluloid flickered by on the eyelid screen). i guess you could say that basically i write out of my ass, not from a music hall-of-fame or r+b or folk or rock or punk throwbacks. not because Cole Porter wasn't a true genius, or Joni Mitchell can say love like Inuits can say snow in 10,000 ways. ok, i do know a little about a few of 'em, my own particular music heroes. still, with rare exception, i don't

know the tune, the singer, the genre or the words. it seems not
to matter all that much. still, it haunts me, my weak excuses for
not knowing those whose work came before and thus i enable
my part-time self-image as a charlatan.

OLD FANS

can identify in my raw face the reflection of the rock dude
in leather pants humping a monitor at the Channel, the Rat,
CBGB's. they connect with a persona and with a band that no
longer has anything to do with me or with what i am working
on now. how do i react? not well. i try to not be rude. i smile
and nod but in the background smirks embarrassed discom-
fort. my first encounter with this phenomenon happened when
i came home my sophomore year from college. it seemed that
many of my high school friends were trying to relocate the person i'd been, the person they remembered but who was no longer wearing those ratty, down-at-the-heel penny loafers. they
seemed to want me to put 'em back on. 'c'mon, Rick. this ain't
you!' in some ways we never change, not deep down. the over-
coat of identity masks the Essential Self from all but the most
observant. we are comfortable in the personality-of-the-present,
but we don't like it if we can't shed skin, if the butterfly can't
liberate itself from the chrysalis. that's why i became distant
at holiday reunions and blamed the hard eyes of old friends
who were convinced i hadn't changed, when, in fact, i had, in
a thousand ways. i refused to be 'read' or i didn't want to be.

my life was covered with hidden bruises and that was part of
the problem. when i seemed to 'not be into girls that much' it
worried my high school pals. they didn't get it or didn't want
to. my new friends at Yale thrived on an honest playing field.
i'd stopped being the make-'em-happy-president-of-the-se-
nior-class boy who knew in his homo heart that he had fooled
everyone, including himself. to be back home was like staring
into a fun house mirror and despising the distortion. and so
it is with fans. even new ones. they like a song i never play
anymore. they treasure, on a dusty shelf, a record i can barely
recall. not long ago i ran into a woman who as a teenager was
fanatically devoted to one of my bands. before shows she'd
appear backstage with some wild object she'd decorated mean-
ingfully and given to us with all her heart. sadly, i not only
failed to recognize her, i had no memory at all of any incident
or interaction or gift. it had all gone down the brain drain.
i felt awful. i did not live up to her nostalgic daydream. i'm
hardly a big shot in the music business. i am, at best, a small
fish in a Jamaica Plain pond, known but not iconic, which
is fine. i like how it is. mostly i like what i'm working on at
present and am well over my archives. so forgive me, whomever you are, if i have that vacant look when you say 'hi,' when
you remember when. i have long since thrown out the leather
pants and the see-thru blouse or the lead vocal stomp. i do sincerely appreciate your postcard recollection. on a rare occasion
when i listen to a record i made 20, 30 years ago, i am moved
by the spew of memories, jokes, arguments, colors and scenes.
one thing does bother me, however. i wonder when it's a guy,

say, in his 40's with kids? 'did i hit on you back then?' because the boy he used to be is now scatter-eyed, losing head hair and has a pig gut. maybe he was fond of the attention. maybe, in retrospect, he'd actually wished i'd tried to get into his pants. or maybe because i didn't, he respected me but worries about his shy son standing just behind him. all of this in my cobwebbed attic over something as shallow as being recognized as The Rick Berlin.

PERFORMING

at nine. first as a cub scout with a wiffle and singing what the grownups were calling in 1954 a 'negro' spiritual...in blackface (burnt cork on grease paint). that was the first time i remember doing anything like this. the unfamiliar rush in my skinny chest in front of a crowd of easy-to-love-you parents. i think i'd seen my dad in The Pirates of Penzance and was bowled over. the lights, color, make-up, huge bellowing voices and pit band killed me, as well as the on-the-road Broadway musicals that hit Philly that i went to with my family. the stage was lit up like a forest fire with dancing, gesticulating, big, busty broads and (did i know it at the time?) gay, gay, gay, chorus boys. what was this? how was i drawn to this flame? this had to have inspired my show-'n-tell boyhood. i'd whip a cape around my shoulders and jump through windows onto the lawn as if to save the day. i busted through a barn wall into a

room-within-a-room and imagined myself Flash Gordon.
i would mind-wander out a third-story window into an oth-
er-personality night sky and fantasize a dream-cloud Neverland to which i belonged. i banged out 'original' piano improvisations at the Prout's Neck talent show. but when it really
took hold was in choir and chorus at the Episcopal Academy.
trying out with my thin reed of a voice, singing scales with
earnest eyebrows and hoping to impress the choir master
with my little boy/girl's voice. which i did, making choir-boy
and chorus-kid. i was exuberant and red-faced in my (brief)
tremulous solo at the Big Moment spring concert. i giggled
in chapel over smothered farts-in-robes, a hard-in-the-pants
morning boner, the boy soprano beside me i called my 'best
friend.' it wasn't just foolin' around. it instigated a transfor-
mative shiver in the soul, all this showing off in front of any
audience. i can't remember a time, since the cub scout Uncle
Remus, when i was not in a play, chorale, glee club or living
room show-and-tell. at Yale my entire social life revolved
around singing groups: the white-tie prestige, the complex
arrangements, the dazzling eyes-that-won't-let-go-of-you
effect on girls and closeted boys, the fat sound—a cappella—
that could fill a hall. i joined choir, glee club, The Duke's Men
and The Whiffenpoofs. we were ginned-up songsters with
tinkling cocktails, leaning against mantle pieces, champagne
badges of courage in a faux-demimonde, an icicle-keening
tenor bounding across a college yard in the autumn frost. sex,
music, art, performance was a steak bomb i ate up. still, i was
singing songs i had not written, that didn't express my inner

or outer life. when, years later, on a borrowed upright in an over-stimulated New Haven house, i began to write my own songs and my own music, a shift occurred. i was not filling another's shoes, but standing in my own. i'm thinking about this now because a friend asked me recently why i perform. i didn't know what to say. i'd never been asked. i hadn't thought about it. Bob Dylan said 'the only time he felt like his real self was on stage' (on stage being more authentic than 'real life'). it is the exact same for me. i am my most-est self when i perform. in captivating ears, eyes and hearts, one imagines an electric synapse with another. one synthesizes his microscopic view of self, life, friends, loss, trauma, love and sex on a safe proscenium, offered up risk free. and then there's The Zone. if you give it all you got, if you 'leave it all on the stage,' you occasionally inhabit an ego-vanishing dimension. your 'you' vaporizes. you transmogrify into an energy that is not from, but through the Self. your 'muse' Ouija-boards an art wave. this is intoxicating and let's face it, you love the love even as you wonder how to win the anonymous heart. you invent reciprocity. the nightmare, the other side of the coin, is the uncertainty that lurks above every singer's watchtower, the hell-possibility of fakery, of when your 'acting and not being' spits on your face. 'who-the-fuck do i think i am? i suck! they hate me! my voice is gross. my songs are horrible! i'm over-doing it. anyone is better at this than i am. i'm wasting your time.' etc., etc.—crash, burn, explode. or when the narcissistic, star-fucking groupie blow-job-staggers past an open door, or when the i-need-to-get-high post-coital sadness storms

in after leaving all your everything on stage, or when the
'intense need to be loved but no one's there' hurls you into the
dank house of horrors—'they loved me minutes ago, where
are they now?' it's lonely at the top (or the bottom), even for a
weekend blues warrior, a fat Karaoke singer, a sweaty shed-
ding teenager with a hard-on in his shorts doing 'moves' in
front of a mirror. for all these reasons, pro or con, i do what i
do on any given night on any stage that will have me. maybe,
like the tenor Jussi Björling or like Mark Sandman, i will drop
dead performing, no regrets, with slow-motion flowers falling
like snow upon the stage.

HEAVEN CAN WAIT

before there was a 'Bat Out of Hell' there was 'Neverland'—a
rock opera by Jim Steinman, directed by Barry Keating and
staged at Amherst College. i never saw it. i was at the Yale
Drama School being a weak, revolutionary hippie—i quit after
a few months a) because i thought they were giving the short
end of the stick to the black kids in my class, b) because this
was my early adventure as a song writer and c) because one
of the dudes at Amherst, a serious dope dealer, has scripted
a movie and wanted me to be in it. this was not a hard decision. the shoot was to take place in Grenada, West Indies,
on a giant 135-foot schooner and we would be given free
rooms to live in, free scooters to shoot around the island on

and all the food and drugs we could swallow—a paradise but that's another story. anyhow, Grenada is where i met Barry and after the movie flamed out (busted for nudity) and we returned home, Barry got in touch with me to audition for 'Neverland' in the big city. sure. why not see where this goes? i was an extremist performer, hauling up at least in my mind, acid references. i remember one improv where i was both bowling ball and pins, knocking myself over with my own rolling self. Richard Gere, at that time a 19-year-old rock singer, was cast as the lead. we actually wrestled in one of the developmental rehearsals and he wasted me. flat. in seconds. but the show fell apart. i moved to Boston, started Orchestra Luna, lost the Epic deal, and started a second OL and it was then that we were asked to be the pit band for yet another attempt at 'Neverland.' as i was not really a proper piano player, i was assigned the part of a killer nun. in rehearsal i jumped off the stage and broke my foot. i lost the part. the show never went up but Steinman signed Karla DeVito to be 'the girl' for the soon to be touring 'Bat Out of Hell' gig, then also tried to get OL's Steven Paul Perry to play guitar. i was elbowed aside and developed strong distrust for what had initially been an innocent career in the biz. my foot still hurts.

¶

BOOZE/DRUGS

"Each time I returned to the bar after an absence it was always the same with them: "where the hell you been? we thought you died!" I was their freak, they needed me to make themselves feel better."
— *Charles Bukowski (My Vanishing Act)*

THE 'REGULAR'

i read in BUTT (as in GAY butt) that that year-of-magical-
drinking singer/performer Kiki (of Kiki & Herb) learned that
not drinking one day a week is good for the kidneys and liver. i
take her advice, although my room mate tells me i don't drink
enough (five watery Miller Lites a night) for any of this to
matter. so what? i give it a shot. i take Sunday off the Lites and
spend it with a book, knees under, pumpkin lampshade overhead feeling 'clean' because those beers at the Behan, midnight
to one, seem dull on day seven and repetitive and when i add
up the time off, it's nearly 48 hours of booze-free life. lo and
behold, the day after is one crystal-clear sky. what i do miss by
walking past, head down—i will not under any circumstance
change my mind and give in—are the big arms of friends,
how they look up when another bum bangs through the door,
the laughs, the farting dogs on leashes, the Red Sox/Patriots/
Celtics/Bruins analysis, the gossip, the nod into the night
from the unknown solo who's not afraid to talk and who wants
to tell his life to a stranger, the cute one at the dark end of the
bar who has me thinking about him when he's not around and
who was so much fun to spar with the night before, even as he
avoids me the next time i look to see if there's that spark in his
eye when he sees me laughing like an idiot over nothing funny.
i miss all that. you see i have never ever been 'regular' at anything. certainly not in any bar. the Behan has pulled me in like
a mafia don, a jolt of blurred reality, the steady unexpected

look from a beautiful boy. it is church, club house, friend and family. it is as regular as i will ever get.

IN THE WEEDS

i first got high in college, my senior year. 'when does it begin?' i wondered. 'i don't notice anything...' i laid back on a filthy dormitory persian rug, closed my eyes and tripped into cartoon land. Daffy Duck quacked at me in a field of sunflowers, leaping and laughing, an animation by Van Gogh. a week later i listened to Horowitz perform Chopin's funeral étude. my mother appeared in a pale, blue, greek robe crossing a cracked Dali desert. her head fell back, freighted with sadness, an exaggerated Picasso profile weeping slow-motion mercury tears. she held my father in her arms, like a baby, his tiny limbs were crooked and blackened like the burnt ends of match sticks. she traversed the landscape in deliberate Martha Graham strides. her movement echoed the dark, basso piano chords Vladimer struck. i was shattered by the visceral hallucination that came on by inhaling this tiny, dried-up plant. it was 1967 and i jumped on the flower power bandwagon. sadly, years later, i got paranoid every time i smoked. i talked too much, i laughed too loudly, i stared too aggressively and hated the high. pot stopped being fun. some wise, old goat on a Cambridge street corner explained that this happens to some of us. that it's physiological. the body reaches a tipping point. the bad outweighs the good. Mary Jane scowls. she's over you. she's moved on. after many more tests to prove him wrong, i gave up. i stopped. no more ganja. no more paranoid nightmares. not for me. in the late 90's a friend came to town. we went to his brother's apartment. the pipe was passed. maybe this time, i hoped. maybe this time my body's cured of its aversion. two puffs later i'm in orbit. i can't shut up. i can't uncross my legs. i'm frozen, babbling and jumping out of my skin. my friend turns to me and says, deadpan: 'you know, Rick, no one is listening to you.' it took every ounce of energy for me to stand up, find a dark empty room, lie down and wait for it to go away. my body once again rejected the high. lately, however, on occasion, with rarely more than one other person, i can handle a one-shot hit and be ok. it's fun again. pissing takes a century and every conversational nuance is brilliant— insight at every corner. i get lost in the face of the beautiful. wow, man, your teeth, your crooked yellow teeth are fuckin' beautiful and the place where your neck disappears into your shirt...

IRISH

even though i work at an Irish bar and spend six nights a week at another, i'm not of the green. not even close. German/ French/Scot is the mutt i am. still, when i think about them, these loud, red-faced boy/men who have become my friends,

i like what i see. i like how hard they work. i like the juice
they give a good story. i like how they laugh from the toes up
and that they know how to sing, gifted or otherwise, balls to
the stinking wall. i admire their healthy regard for death, the
ritual of the wake, of seeing the body, of bidding farewell and
drinking ferociously-to-the-memory-of. i respect their reluc-
tance to open up, to deliver the dark secret of the self. however,
once you earn their trust, the connection is unbreakable. they
have your back and you theirs, end of story. loyalty is the Bible
and you don't fuck with it. likewise, the pub is their church,
a clubhouse of celebration, belonging, wound-nursing and
absurdity. of course it's the Irish 'disease,' the alcohol fixation,
that gets called out. booze kills, grows a liquor nose, ruins
families, makes liars and lousy fathers—the all-too-familiar
list of debilitation. on the other hand, one can't help but envy
these blokes and broads and their athletic bouts of drinking: a
pint in a slobbery mouth, numbing away a shitty day, a clink
of the glass to a good joke, forcing an ugly shot down a reluctant throat, jacking up enough courage to make a move on the
snotty bitch at the end of the bar and so it goes. here lies an
exuberance that has no twin in any culture i can think of. we
WASPs have our fussy martinis and wry smiles. in Paris, the
little finger rises like a baby penis, a prissy sniff of fine wine.
the Japanese shatter themselves silly in safe houses of repute
but practice daytime decorum with perfect samurai hair. vodka
ripped Russians tend to fight each other as much as the Irish,
but are dour, pasty-faced and depressive. Hispanics know how
to party but don't, near as i can tell, genuflect at the gate of the

corner pub. these Irish own the map. they throw back booze
with an abandon that is as childlike as it is insane. i for one
can't keep up. four or five puny Miller Lites and i'm kaput. add
a sickening shot and my mouth hangs open like a fuck doll.
these guys, these shit-faced Irish hounds achieve that rare
rubbery gift of a good sentence, a lacerating point of view, a
sudden jerked-open window of insight no matter how many
sheets to the wind. the other night is a case in point: two
bartenders from the Brendan Behan (named after the famous
alky/poet himself and hung with portraits of Irish writers and
drunkards) share that rarest of rejoicings: a double birthday,
same exact. 'he has my brain,' says one. the other is jumping
up and down on a bar bench, squinty-eyed, spewing beer like
piss onto the floor, lost in a parallel universe. back from crowd
surfing at a Pogues concert, back to the Behan kite high, out-
of-body happy and full of arrgh, they kill the rasta oiling out
of the speakers, crank up the Pogues, link arms in a scrum
and sing; the loudest lung work i've heard since the fat lady
sang in '04 and the Yankees watched hell freeze over. i don't
know any of the songs but they they rope me in nevertheless.
i nod like Hillary Clinton as they shout out, nose to ceiling, a
cluster-fuck of bellowing cross-eyed lions. my outsider identity dissipates as they explode these glorious, raging songs.
it doesn't matter that i can't join in. fuck that. i love every
awkward minute. they eye each other like dogs who'd spent
the day chasing a rabbit down a hole. this is not stereotypi-
cal male bonding. no sir. it's more like a fist of 21st century
Captain's Blood riding a Kamikazi rocket into an Irish worm

hole. this double birthday beams the rest of us up. i break
away and return to the bar for my weak-assed Miller Lite and
my periscope view of the crowd—the boy scan. meanwhile
the joint is on its feet rocking in a frenzy of song or blinking
from an uptight distance, missing out entirely. the 'best night
of my life, ever' says one. i look him in the eye just to be sure
he means it. of course he does. how many of those can you
count on one hand? and damned if you don't need to be Irish
to know the fookin' difference. CODA: i run into a Behan rat
who'd been off the sauce for a week. 'how's it going?' i ask.
'great! i feel great!' 'really?' i say. 'how come?' 'i know a guy
with pills.' 'pills?' 'yeah.' 'what kind?' 'Xanax.' 'oh...i see. cool.'

COKE + A CAN O' COKE

i was at the Rat in the early 80's watching some hot guy band.
the kid next to me was bobbing his head arhythmically. he
looked like a young Ric Ocasek but not as string-bean long
and drawn out. he said he was from Peru or some west coast
South American country. he had black hair, shiny black eyes
and a bright smile. i asked him back to the house (my boyfriend was away doing God-knows-what with God-knows-
whom—we both played that game). 'sure,' he said. 'you wanna
do some kawcaine?' he explained in broken english that he
had a profitable connection with a drug cartel in his country
and that he was dealing the stuff to 'all de beeg bahnds in
town.' 'would eew like to try some?' i'd never done a single

line but hey, why not give it a shot; he seemed to like me and
who knew where this would lead? back at the apartment he
broke out a stamp-sized packet of powder, cut it with a credit
card, rolled a 100 dollar bill, snorted two fat lines and handed
me the tube (all the 80's cliches). i'd watched him do it and
followed suit. it shot up my nose like a dental drill and i got
instantly horny. we were in the guest room (a nod to false
propriety). he lay on his back, sneakers off, chain smoking. we
had a couple of Cokes in cans on a side table. he was tapping
ashes into the tin keyhole and squeezing stubs into the brine.
he was coke-stoked for sure, but i wasn't hip to all the signs.
he had a sweet oblivion in his eyes that erased any walls he
might have had about who i was or what i might be up to
with him. i touched his leg, his knee and he didn't budge. he
closed his eyes, opened his mouth a little and stopped talking.
i unbuckled his belt, pulled his zipper, brought it out like a
fish and went down. he was right-away hard, beautiful there
but i had dry mouth. it felt like i was sucking bark. i needed to
get slippery, to drink. i held him with my left hand and took
a frantic swig of Coke from what i thought was my set-aside
can. it wasn't. it was his. it was filled with tobacco. sloshing
down the hopper were two cigarette butts and globs of ash.
it went down and back like a zip gun and i puked all over the
kid's belly in a gusher. if this was his 'first time with a guy,'
it was probably going to be the last. he grabbed the pillow,
swiped the vomit, yanked up his tight black jeans, click-locked
the belt, collected his coke gear and hurtled down the stairs.
i saw him off but didn't get him off and never saw him again.

maybe he located some non-projectile head from one of boys from one of 'da beeg bahnds in town.' who cares? i'm flipping out. what had i done? why was this drug pounding my heart like a Gatling gun. hmm...i thought, why not run it off? that ought to do the trick. i sprinted back upstairs, dragged on some filthy running shorts and took off, thomping the pavement like a duck just as the sun came up. sweat pimpled my face and my fists pumped like pistons. of course the symptoms intensified. i was scared. i called my boyfriend who, unbeknownst to me was doing the same thing with some colt in Jersey but i knew that he knew about coke, knew all about it. he told me to stop running, to take a shower and to wait 'til the dark fear passed. in a few short months he'd be dealing the shit himself and terminating our dead-in-the-water relationship and our band at the time. coke is good for that. 'instant asshole' a friend calls it. no shit, Tonto.

CHINESE BOX

MSG floats like a brown cloud in the bar. i'm having a beer with friends. a clot of indie lesbians is chowing down, chopsticks like knitting needles, pigging out from an open box (one of those ear-flap chinese take-out origamis crammed with sweaty unknowns). they gin up the gossip as the odor overtakes the nose the same way fumes from a cartoon pie on a window sill sniffs Goofy off the ground. but we're lazy and won't skitter across Centre St to grab last call at Food Wall. strangely, out of the hazy blue, a tattooed, pierced-into-oblivion boi grl appears beside me, food-box mouth agape and held under my nose. 'want some?' she smiles. it's chock full of those stapled-tight peking dumpling pillows, a food offer i can't refuse. 'sure,' i say, as calmly as possible, taking hold of the bottom end of the shiny white paper lotus. 'thanks, babe.' i'm thinking she wants me to eat the entire box or at least to share the pillows with my friends, but as i pull it towards my lap, she pulls back. i pull again, thinking she's being careful not to spill the pillows, but she pulls harder: back and forth, to and fro, a miniature war of wills. oh...i get it. she's offering up just one of the dumplings, one only and wants to navigate the room, handing out the rest one-at-a-time to the remaining rats. she's upset. her eyebrows are arm wrestling. we're locked in gay combat as if my hand has yet to get the brain telegram: LET GO OF THE FUCKING BOX, ASSHOLE! at long last my greedy truck driver fingers relax, she retrieves the goods and crabs away in a spitfire huff. i guess i busted her PC share-the-wealth goodwill big time. my bad.

VAMPIRE AT THE BAR

a Polaroid: the kid is super Michael Jackson-y with pow-der-white face, Baby Jane Hudson-red lips in a smear, corn yellow teeth, layer cakes of black something-or-other denim,

goth cape accoutrement. who is this Captain Midnight who
rides the stool at the end of the bar at the end of the world
seconds before last call? should i, would i, four beers in the
pocket, strike up the band? i need to hear a sound, an emana-
tion, a gesture, a cough, a clue? i need something to give him
away, to set me up with an angle to hit on. while i'm throwing
my can-i-buy-you-a-beer-where-are-you-from-do-you-smoke-
pot resume together i see, in one dark corner, a familiar face,
an almost-but-not-quite...friend. i think there's a Tanqueray
'n tonic sparkling in one upraised claw. we share the loud
gay laugh, have a similar over-the-glasses view of life, of odd
behaviors and friends in common but don't know each other
well. the point being: as i perch three stools to the left of the
dark drifter, casing him out with a whale's eye, i twist and cast
a lighthouse lamp across the joint and see my friend waving.
oh, i get it. he is captivated. he has an interest in Iago. i twirl
back and see that Mr. Spellbound-by-his-own-monologue has
two blokes giving fascinated unconditional attention. the voice
is lispy, an alto. eew. the relief i feel at being turned off (knowing i won't have to take a fool's stab) is palpable. a sigh of the
body. it is then that my friend from the corner has mounted
the stool next to mine and stares like a bird dog at Zorro. the
bartender asks if he needs a drink. 'oh no, i'm here to see my
friend Rick,' he purrs, eyes lasered onto Hamlet, who is collecting his black shoulder bag, black iPhone, black everything
and heading out the door. 'here to see, Rick?' i scoff. 'you are
so full of shit.' 'that obvious, huh?' 'are you kidding!?' (like
next-door-neighbor housewives hanging laundry and gossip-

ing, the bond of fensterkaufers—Isherwood Deutsch for 'window shoppers'). 'i think i've seen my first vampire,' he says. one wonders if one should allow oneself to be entertained by a total stranger in black who might nip you in the neck and who might have been reading up on the Craigslist Killer. he hasn't been back.

IT IS DRUNK

a girl slid off a bar stool at Doyle's and melted into the floor, her unsteady, lean-on-whatever's-within-reach hobble to the exit was in slo-mo and hysterical to watch. i put my hand on a table as i choked back a laugh. the poor thing had no clue. tomorrow morning she'll be 'sick.' i sat next to an off-the-boat Irish kid at the Behan who had seven empty pints of Guinness in front of him lined up like clay ducks. as he was counting and gulping and midway through #8 i asked, 'how can you get away with this and not be out cold?' 'i'm tough,' he squinted. as soon as he drained the last pint his head hit the bar like a brick. an older woman drinking giant buckets of cheap merlot was ok until she ordered 'just one more tiny, li'l glass.' her phrasing clear as day until, when i checked back, i got this: 'erm moumph frun grad ur.' she had crossed the slur river into Neanderthal. an octogenarian and Very Proper Lady in low heels, a sparkly blouse with exaggerated eyeliner (improperly applied and smeary) was on her way to the ladies room. one heel cracked under foot. she grabbed a railing in the nick of time. a waitress asked if she was all right. 'i'm fine,' she insisted, 'just a wee bit tipsy.' 'tipsy' paddled her way into the loo and the waitress rolled her eyes, 'tipsy?! my ass. she's hammered!' funny how we pretend we're not destroyed when everyone else can see that we are. just try to convince a drunk he's been shut off for his own good. he'll go ballistic. if they're cute you put up with the vomit potential in hopes of a score but inevitably pretty becomes not so pretty and you make your way home alone. on the other hand, one lame night in a glitzy bar in Amsterdam called 'It' as in 'look at it, she's gorgeous!' i'm drinking and staring and hoping and worked up all at once in this Dutch playground crammed to the gills with the young and the hot. a skateboard hero with a watercolor mustache was so drunk he was propped up like an abandoned doll: his legs hung wide, his arms weighed a ton, his hands were engorged. he slouched against a mirror wall, nursing a vodka. every thirty seconds he belched. you could tell because his cheeks puffed out, 'bluh.' his lips were parted and slippery behind a puke pout, puke breath, puke skin. one chartreuse bubble floated sadly in front of his Novocaine face. i wanted to rip his clothes off but i kept to myself. it wouldn't go over big at 'It.' it is drunk.

SPEED BUMP

i usta hit it hard in Philly when i was imagining myself an architect. accepted by the Yay-ul Architecture School on a full ride i was thinking, well, i'm sort of an artist on the inside but i need to make a living so maybe something like designing pretty buildings would do the trick and balance inner artist with outer realist. recon: i got a job with Vincent G. Kling and Associates in downtown Philly. i labored over floor plans and carefully measured toilet placement. at night, however, i'd get high on anything i could get my hands on—hash, weed, lsd, mushrooms, peyote, sunflower seeds, meth. loved the double life. a favorite junket was to drop a pill, drive to the airport, park at the end of the runway behind the chain link fence and watch planes take-off and land. big bellied sky whales lifted your hair and crushed your eardrums. or we'd hit up the Electric Factory (a Rat-sized venue at the time) where i lucked-out and saw Hendrix ride a greased pig onto the stage in front of a crowd of 20, or Iron Butterfly zone off into a San Francisco twilight, or Three Dog Night with their hairy chests scream out "One Is The Loneliest" into battered mikes. i traipsed up to the skinny, androgynous bassist from the west coast band Spirit, shook his limp hand (a forefinger grazing my palm in code) and gazed like a teenage girl into his mercury eyes. all this hurled me into the day-job cell-block at work where i'd sketch four-by-eight foot posters (faux-Peter Max) and color them in with a fist of psychedelic magic markers and which

pre-dated my first bad trips on meth. i loved the initial rush,
the humorless solve-all-the-problems-of-the-world edge,
heart beating like a hummingbird. it was awesome until the
inevitable crash. i would denounce to myself all the hot ideas
that only minutes ago were 'genius.' i hated the sound of my
voice. my skin crawled with invisible bugs. my eyes dried up.
the only solution would be, though i didn't have any in those
days, a sedative or put-you-to-sleep weed. more often than
not i was stuck sweating it out. long hours of self-loathing
and suicidal panic. it did help on cross country drives. who
needed sleep? after a brief incarceration in a Santa Barbara
jail (for shoplifting), i was losing it. i didn't know who to
call. somehow my friend Harlow (back in Philly) was able to
persuade my infuriated Old Man to dole out the dough to fly
him out and drive me home. on meth. no stops necessary. with
Tucker—my black lab—passed out in back on doggy tranquilizers we drove straight 'cross country in sixty hours. if we
got tired, we ate more speed. in Missouri we hit a pit stop at
an over-sized, barn-like Jesus restaurant—early afternoon and
practically empty except for Harlow and me and a round table
of little old ladies playing bridge. they didn't even look at us.
their tight little shoulder blades fluttered like insects's wings
trying to disregard the loud, obnoxious hippies in the corner,
banging glasses and yelling at the waitress. i was in the john
taking a long piss when i cut this explosive cannonball fart.
i'd left the door open to the men's room and the entire restaurant heard it. the bridge ladies couldn't cope. cards sputtered
up into the air and away from their precise gnarled angry

little hands...sppwoosh! and we never cut the meth talk for
the entire drive. we solved all the problems of our love lives,
poverty, war, inequity on the 2.5 day jaunt. once home, we
fell apart, helplessly fucked up in a 100 mph daze. i gave the
shit up soon thereafter only to replace it down the rock 'n
roll highway with coke. more glamorous than speed, it was
sexy—the cutting, shaping, snorting. the encrusted mirror
passed back and forth across the table with a one-time-only
persuadable. the horny rush would subtract all moral code and
inhibition. but that too, like its white trash pal, would induce
a grotesque fall from grace. good and bad times they were,
those dark days of infantile fear and loathing.

¶

E M O / S E X

"One only loves that which one does not possess entirely."
— S. Beckett

"...and so it was once upon a time I stood up and broke,
as if by a magical act, the evil curse of obsession. From
that day on...I could abandon completely...to the beauty
of the day, to the joys of the day. It seemed a miracle but
it was the result of many years of struggle, of analysis,
of passionate living...of many people, may places, many
loves, many creations. From that point on I experience
emotional dramas which pass like storms and leave
peace behind."
— Anais Nin

LOVE IS JUST EMOTION ON THE MAKE

my pale, white, old-man, pulpy legs hang overboard, off
my roof as i shout across to you on yours, the alley canyon
between us is too far to jump. i wouldn't anyway. my naked
heel depresses the rubber tar surface and leaves a Robinson
Crusoe's 'Friday' foot impression on a black sand beach. if you
smile i can't see it through the gauze of this bloodshot night
even with the haze of a fat yellow moon. you gesture with
nicotine fingers (the hot, orange tip circling like the manic
gesture of a Bette Davis drag queen). watery emotional voices
sloppy with booze make me wonder about Everything all over
again as i draw another blank. in a snap i could sit next to
you, but best not. not tonight. like housewives yakking across
a line of sheeted laundry we're safe if not sound. your black
pant legs end in damp, sockless sneakers off the edge of our
rooftop dock-o'-the-bay. i click a picture that's too dark to
register. the bell-clinking of ice in a glass is worth the whole
damn night.

REFLECTIONS IN GOLDEN EYES (PUT ANOTHER WAY: PORN SAVES A SEXLESS NIGHT)

this is not a lament. it really isn't. it's just that after a certain point, a certain age, we succumb to gravity. we have no choice. all the jogging and lifting and diets in the world lose that battle. evaporating gradually is the end game of a smooth, handsome face, tight under-chin, lean upper-arms, hammock-less under-eyes and fabulous hair. we cut ourselves loose from the possibility of Something Ever Happening With A Future (i.e. 'a relationship') and rationalize the 'freedom' of it. our surface Self, the one we mock with false modesty, loses its persuasive allure. we let it go. we have to. instead we employ the brutal truth, honesty as a con, our 'charming' seduction repertoire transmogrified into the quiet qualities of The Listener. youth ('the only true aphrodisiac' –Rene Ricard) stops checking us out and looks to others. i remember my mom, Jane Kinscherf, trying on wigs to hide the hair that had fallen out after weeks of chemotherapy. 'God, i look so old!' her vanity vaguely intact but shrugged off in the end with a laugh. it's more weird than sad, her old face refusing to recognize itself, hallucinating a younger version through the impressionistic gauze of squinted eyes. inevitably, deep down, we're pretty sure that we remain that same compelling, fascinating, oddball soul we've always been. we still have much to ask, to give, to love

and to be funny about. but today, at the onset of our greeting
card 'sunset years' we reinvent the way we love. it is no longer
about the chase, about roping someone in, or having them
'see' us. it's about seeing them in a way that serves their needs
and not our own centrifugal neuroses. there's no preparing for
this. no text to teach or Romance for Old Dummies to thumb
through. late love has its own slow momentum and moral
impetus. the beautiful, unreachable, untouchable boy loves us
when he feels like it, not as any flattering sexual fantasy but
because he senses understanding in our hooded eyes. 'this
one has traveled the long love road.' Uncle Awareness is The
Man (our new vanity). the beloved and the ancient sleep side
by side, goat man beside shepherd boy undisturbed on some
bright Kazantzakis Mediterranean island where beings merge
without ownership or showboat passion.

OBSESSION IS A PLAYER

i am adrift in the face, eyes, hands, body, cock, balls, bush, ass,
'soul' of a person. i'll call him A. i wake up to thoughts of him.
i go to sleep the same way. never out of mind though out of
sight. we don't spend a lot of time together, but when we do
there is a lock on the chord between us that no noise, conversation or view can interrupt. this is of course nothing new
in my life, or his. but when the magnifying glass positions
itself above the heart and soul of the beloved, all else recedes.

obsession is a focus as scary as the face on a ninth inning closer. predictably, after months of A, B takes his place. it isn't a rapid transition or fickle but the more time i spend with B, the more i lose track of A. divergent lives, divergent worlds and the revolving romantic door dislodges he who was once all consuming. soon B supersedes A in all areas. i don't see A at all until one night he unexpectedly appears backstage. i don't recognize him. i can't-for-the-life-of-me remember his name. i am shocked. not even his fucking name! who is this, i wonder? who the fuck is this guy who seems to know me so well? the pattern is a cyclical and a cynical one: A overtaken by B who, not soon after though i can't remember when, is replaced by C. a love whore is what i am.

THE LOVE LOTTERY

don't get me wrong, i like Sorella's. there's something about it. it's not quite a diner and is hardly an uppity café. the food can be sketchy. in June a kid was found puking his omelette into the gutter. you have to be smart about what you order. eggs over easy, lukewarm home fries, dark toast with bacon usually gets the job done. the coffee is hardcore, a surefire diuretic promising the inevitable tippy-toe walk to the toilet or a sprint back home with your fingers pressed like a prayer against your sphincter. my favorite thing is to go there alone, on Sunday, eat something safe, read and inventory the young

and incredible. last week they sat me upstairs. i prefer the
original room with the ugly Greek art and omelette signs,
but i don't really care. the big guy who waits on me, thighs
chafing against thighs, is a scenic view in and of himself.
oddly, there is not One Single Handsome Person in sight
which is fine, making it easier to concentrate on my book.
i live on the edge and order a vegetable crêpe with a side of
braised tempeh. it arrives tepid and dull-tasting and the crêpe
the big guy smacks down is spilling over with fruit. i didn't
order fruit, but i refuse to make a scene (we waiters never
want to make a fuss or embarrass a comrade). soon, however,
the big man returns with the veggie version: raw onion, raw
sprouts, damaged spinach in a cold crêpe. i wolf it down. i'm
in a good mood. my noir novel (The Dead Yard – McKinty)
is clickity-clacking down the track. i get lost in it and in the
dead backyard on my plate until, simultaneously, two couples
are seated on either side of my table. the girls are as striking
as the boys. my eyes lift furtively from the page. the kid facing
me on my left has black, briary Brezhnev eyebrows, corn-blue
eyes and full lips, as if lipstick-engorged. he and his girl spend
hours lost in each other's eyes. they have that wet just-show-
ered-after-a-morning-fuck hair, thick and heavily scented
from post-coital cum (my imagination is off the charts). he
smiles as i lurch up from the table to leave, a stack of singles
under my coffee cup. i ask, nervously, if he's seen Rushmore.
he has. 'you look like that kid,' i say, with a big ingratiating
smile. 'no kidding?' it's safe to connect on a silly pretense.
but it is the boy to my right that knocks the breath out of

me. i stare at his legs, Beardsley profile, wild art school hair, big boots. i must look like an uptight sex-starved librarian. i picture him in boxer shorts, peek-a-boo boner, a cliché porn fantasy. what's most captivating is what he and his girlfriend are doing: taking turns drawing on a single napkin. that's right, drawing, with a blunt golf score pencil. she is engrossed as he looks on. it is as if she traces a line on his naked back, in the sun, on the beach sending a shiver up his spine. she pushes the paper over. it's his turn. i try to see what the images are. i'm guessing they're hieroglyphs of a personal, in-joke nature. i can't tell. it doesn't matter. it is this thing between them, this euphoric, sandbox way of liking each other that is beautiful. i love them for it. is she French? she has that Paris-girl, Band of Outsiders vibe with no makeup, pouty lips, a sexy overbite, disheveled hair and who-cares clothes. they are lost in the game. they have won the love lottery.

GAY SCHMAY

the jury is out on this one although i'd expect to get life in the closet from my gay peers. in my head flicker out-takes of The Worst Cliché Images of Homos (e.g. the documentary 'Do I Sound Gay?'). they are worse even than those of some sicko, radical born-against. through my judgmental binoculars 'they' squeal, hiss, walk funny (quick tiny penguin steps) and perform outrageous 'flaming' gestures that sometimes amuse me but most of the time drive me crazy. that is, unless they're

my friends. if not, they're catalogued on my self-righteous
altar, collecting judgement dust. oh no, i tell myself, this is not
internalized homophobia, nor masked self-loathing. i LIKE
myself. i like my queer, gay, poofter, flouncy, faggoty self.
i can be that way, they cannot or i won't approve. i certainly
won't be attracted to them. this reaction rears its ugly head
like the pinkie finger in La Cage Au Folles, all by itself. i can't
help it. i realize how dated this is, how dated i am, zeroing in
on the parade float with the leather boys letting it all hang
out of assless chaps. on the flip side are the on-the-street-
homos i walk past here at home who are as hard to identify as
the metro-sexual straights in the what's-going-on-here local
bar. i'm as often off with my gay-dar as on. however, when
i walk up commercial street in P-town, it hits me all over
again. there they are, the too-tanned, short-shorted shrieking
pansies ogling anyone within eye-shot just to get attention.
the elders (like myself) look with impotent lust at the young,
the cute and the out and proud as if they'd missed something
back in the day. this makes me want to run, to take the New
Year's vow my friend Peter took back in '85 and 'go back in
the closet' because he'd had it with the homos, the culture,
the silliness and the emphasis on surface beauty, youth, ass...
which would of course be the last thing any of us need: more
hiding, more suicides, more beatings, more killings, more
prejudice. still i wonder, are we people first, queer second? do
i ask as a preemptive question of my straight friends if they're
straight? is that the way they introduce themselves: 'hi. i'm
Tom. i'm straight.' no, they don't. there's no need. meanwhile

the outrageous queen makes it known for miles how different she is. look at me. i'm here, i'm queer, i'm fabulous... but
she deserves to, doesn't she? or he? deserve to be who they
are, hell or high water, tutu or sleek couture, punk purple or
tranny? come on already, girlfriend, get over your snotty self.
don't beat around the bush. you're a fag. you always have been.
your sexual orientation that took you however-long to admit
to yourself, to your friends, to the world, is now your badge
of honor, your cred, your artsy mystique. use it, baby. use it to
seduce. 'weird homo voo doo' a kid once called it. don't pull
that 'weird homo voo doo shit on me' he said. as if that would
insinuate me into his pants. still, it baffles, all of it. because i
long to just quiet down all the hissing, cruising, gesticulating
steam and stares and just talk for a bit about anything besides
movie reviews or clothes or who's doing whom. ok, i do all
those things. so yeah, maybe i'm the most egregious example
of the self-hating homo. but there you have it. c'est moi. i prefer the ambiguous bars where my predatory instinct feels at
least in the murky pool of impossibility, possible. that conversation may or may not lead to intimacy but will at least spool
out a thread of contact that does not necessarily lead to deed,
but at least to connection. but what's up with that? my friend
Danny (scorer of infinite boys) claimed: 'it's sex or love, baby'
and not both. so where am i? i guess i identify with the Beats,
with Ginsberg, where love finds a home in dark places, in
friendship, in art. his affliction being his continuous, obsessive
attachment to straight boys. i'm with you there, Allen, dark it
can be. deep, dark and beautiful.

RIMBAUD, REDUX

you know the question: what is your type? you can sort-of
answer that, but don't want to. you don't want to admit to
anyone, least of all yourself, that you have a type, or worse, a
pattern. but go on, Berlin, you can say. you like the marginal,
the terrified, scary adolescents or near to, the ex-jailbirds, the
ones who hurt inside, scratch poetry on napkins and throw
'em away, the dispossessed, the dark and the lonely. it's not
like any old crumpled-up ferocious kid will do. yours is not
some easily-tagged Florence Nightengale syndrome. they
have to be good looking in that pimply, seering-eyed way.
they have to see through my bullshit. they have to be young
and pretentious and smart. ('we ALWAYS think they're
smart' – Danny Fields). when i look back at these boys, especially reading, again, about Rimbaud, i realize they all have
some of him in them. some more than others. as i have some
of Verlaine in myself. more than once have they enthralled me,
set me on edge and turned me inside out and far away from
complacency. among these, most of all, was Michael, the boy i
met at the screen door of my sister's apartment in Somerville.
there he stood, in his underwear, out of the blue, panting from
the run from his house. 'will you walk me home?' he asked. i
had never met him, never laid eyes on him before this night.
'sure.' of course i would. we were inseparable for the next year
and the next and the next. he looked like Rimbaud. he had the
same challenging, piercing, ice-blue eyes. he wrote prayers

and poems and burned them. he aimed a gun at the back of his
father's head when they walked in the woods in Louisiana. the
gun was loaded and he almost pulled the trigger. he was only
12. from his porch he saw a motorcyclist beheaded when his
bike slid under the tailgate of a truck. he wrote love words on
the wall of his bedroom with his dog's shit. he threw matches
into the brush alongside a narrow road on Martha's Vineyard.
it caught fire. he drove my friend's VW into the ocean. he
took off his clothes and boarded a metro bus stark naked. he
gave me a black eye after sex. he shoved a Coke bottle up his
dog's asshole. we slow danced in a bar for old timers, hugging,
near kissing, showing off and laughing. they smiled at us. it
was his idea. he dropped acid with me but because he ground
his teeth, or thought he did, he refused ever after to close
his mouth. it hung open and drooled. i suppose he was crazy.
of course i think we all are, but it was all too much for him
and for me. i met someone else and he was hurt. 'we always
hurt the ones we love.' at a friend's suggestion he went to a
camp for tough kids up in Maine. the kids thought he was
gay. i guess he'd made a sloppy pass at one of them. i'm not
sure, but the short of it was that he got hit in the lower back
with a log and damaged his spleen. it was removed. when he
returned home he had a scar like a railroad track on his belly.
then things got worse. his mom didn't know what to do. he
wound up in Marlboro State Mental Hospital. when i went
to see him he was standing in line, in a regulation pale-blue
pair of pajamas, accepting his paper cup of pills just like the
patients in One Flew Over the Cuckoo's Nest. a few days later

he drowned himself in a hospital bathtub. it was a scandal. he was not being watched. i went to his funeral. the boys from the camp in Maine carried his coffin. he looked beautiful at the wake, even though he'd put on weight. i broke down. his mom told me that no one in his life had loved him as much as i had. still, i wonder, i worry to this day, that it was our, my, tidal-wave attraction to him that hurt him most. that sent him over the cliff. i still love him, my Rimbaud. he never found the African desert. he never found peace, or gentle love. since Michael, there have been others—two former inmates, an artist who again, resembles the dangerous one, a fire-starter of the soul, a ridiculer, a prescient. my knees buckle every time they seem to find me.

NEVERLAND

'i'm too old for this.' i hear it all the time, even from people younger than me. the sense that what was once funny or do-able or easy now feels used up, jaded, is-that-all-there-is? 'i can't do it anymore.' what are they missing? the up-all-night drinking, waitressing for shitty tips from asshole customers, loving the mirror or, most embarrassing, going for The One after years of disappointment? to hell with it, throw in the towel, fuck this shit. sound familiar? as for me, jowled, eye-bagged and slack-mouthed, i don't feel it, not yet. even with skin problems, flu shots, stringy hair, hearing loss, lower back pain, hemorrhoids and insomnia and the goal posts more in focus then ever. i still feel like a kid, a 70-year-old kid with a squinting eye-on-self and a forgiving (blind?) ambivalence. i laugh at how much older i look in the mirror than i feel. in many ways i haven't grown up. i don't have a Big Boy Job (30+ years of waitressing is more fun than money and has no ladder-to-climb future). i don't shoulder a wife and kids. i don't own a house. i don't have a for-real get-in-the-way-of-selfish-routine boyfriend. it's a relief we can't see ourselves behaving. we would, i would for sure, be horrified. watching the music videos my friends shot for Old Stag was like staring at a stranger. i LOOK like that?! what the fuck! when i per-form or waddle around Doyle's or have animated talks at the Behan i imagine that i look what? 45? tops? lithe, no spastic facial contortions, bright eyes, wise wit. Jean Cocteau, during the filming of La Belle et la Bete, ran about, hung sheets, adjusted arms on the walls holding candles and observed: 'we felt like teenagers until we saw ourselves in the mirror and realized that we were old men.' is the surface a lens to the soul? not if you're really looking, but who is? old folks out for dinner, sparkly-eyed, who need a cane to shuffle across the floor and have a date with the boob tube later, seem to harbor a covert hankering for deep throat or a dirty poem from an imploring suitor or an honest kiss even as they assemble in awkward dignity their minefield of propriety. a friend of mine emails: 'America is no country for old men.' the crusty, useless, annoying elderly out-to-pasture, no longer jacked-up with rampant hard-ons have run out of turf. 'i'm too old for this.'

and yet, inside, under the surface, are we not all ageless? does our skin, our voice, our walk give us away? did Peter Pan have it right, or Dorian Gray?

O TANNENBAUM

i'd fallen asleep. there were only 6, 7 people left in the living room still drunk from the party, our annual Christmas party, the surreal Christmas party. the pretty lights, the stench of pine and beer and pot and debris all over the kitchen. that's when the tree fell over. it just leaned and fell, slo-mo, balls cracking on the floor like eggs, the lights twisted like under-wear around the bulbous waist of the tree. the Wiccan star was toppled and replaced with a can of PBR jammed onto the hard thrusting tippy top. it looked hung-over leaning against the window. we lifted her up, yanked off the can, straightened the lights, swept up the broken balls and re-inserted and tightened the stand screws. it was ok now, but off kilter. room-mate Travis: 'the Christmas tree has been drinking, not me...' now it has a personality, being at a tilt. more endeared am i to this one, this imperfect touchstone to childhood, than all the pretty houses with all their pretty trees. pretty loses out to truth. the next night is a dead zone at work, but i luck out. two Very Cute Boys (Berklee/LA) are among the few seated in my section. because it's slow going, we talk. i, on shaky legs, the power of The Beautiful upseting my balance. the

black-haired kid in particular hurts to look at. i have to latch
onto words like a plank in a flood in order to not hold his eyes
uncomfortably. to be with both and not monopolize one vs the
other and without presuming intimacy. all goes nicely. info
is exchanged as if after a car accident, smiles all round and
nervous goodbye handshakes. we meet up later at the Behan.
the rush rising with each sentence. i stumble. my stumbling
is obvious i'm sure to these straight, savvy kids. they know
i'm a homo, they know that i know that they know. but here's
the kicker—drunken tree part two BEFORE i see the boys at
the Behan. there's a group that hits Doyle's after the Berklee
boys leave. they came from volunteering at a homeless shelter.
they and the homeless with them are Not Cute. some stink,
their faces have bruises, there are holes in their clothes and
their shoes are untied. they are persnickety about food orders,
although joyful and full of legit Christmas spirit. they sing in
loud, out-of-tune voices all the carols they can remember and
then standards ('Puff the Magic Dragon,' 'Kum-By-Ya') up
on their feet, hugging and singing at each other. i skate back
and forth from bar to table, cleaning up, delivering food and
beer when one of them, the dirtiest, with pockmarked skin, a
sweaty scarf, open boots unlaced, shirt-tails out, orders one
Bud bottle after another. as soon as i drop one off, he asks
again. when the singing really takes over, he goes to the bar
and orders a bigger beer, a giant bottle of Pilsner Urquell. he
isn't going back. he isn't going to be part of the silly singing.
he sits by himself at a round table with his big green bottle
staring into space. during one of my manic traverses, he looks

up at a spot above my head and says 'i love you.' his lipless
mouth agape, a yawning walrus with flappy chops and the
faint lift of a smile. 'i love you,' wow. had Very Cute said this
to me from his astonishing face i would have collapsed into
his heart. i am, like the song says, a fool for beauty. but this
homeless man, like our peculiar, sad tree, is the one to deliver
this snail of an endearment. not the pretty boy with the hot
smarts, nor his friend with the dark eyes.

PISS ETIQUETTE

the men's room is wall-to-wall dudes. i can't hold it another
second. i sneak into the ladies' room. it's empty. it's not what
i'm used to. here are immaculate stalls, a wisp of perfume, a
tampon dispenser, sparkly mirrors, a smear of lipstick on a
faucet and a baby rack. i imagine gossip zinging around the
tiles, dishing the bitches back in the bar. the opposite is true
of the men's room. sloppy urinals flecked with pubic hair, beer
bottles, puke stains, unraveled, damp toilet paper and stink-o
stalls with graffiti ads for blow jobs and, most importantly,
no talk. we're not supposed to. the difference is behavioral.
guys in public johns observe The Unspoken Rules. 1) don't go
in there with the guy you're hanging out with, he will wait
for you at the bar, or at your table, keeping watch over your
cell phone and wallet and wait, properly, until you return,
alone, so that he can then, on his own, relieve himself. you

don't talk about it. you just do it. 2) if there are more than
two urinals and one is occupied, do not take the slot next to
the other guy. use the stall or keep an empty piss hole safely
between yourself and your neighbor. 3) don't talk. talking
implies weird friendliness in an unfriendly location. 4) it's ok
to fart, but if you're a big, barking-tuba farter, don't laugh or
draw undue attention. keep your reaction to yourself. farts are
not funny in the men's room. just fart and get the fuck outta
there. 5) flush with your foot, elbow or knee. do not use your
hand. you never know what insidious herpes sore has smeared
itself onto the chrome. 6) do not, under any circumstance, look
at the person next to you. stare at the ceiling, focus on the
golden yarn squirting into the porcelain or pick your nose,
but do not look. that said of course, we do. we all do. we look.
we don't look like we're looking, but that wandering falcon
eye surveillance radar works overtime. so, yeah, we do it. we
look. we don't want to be caught looking, we don't look all the
time, but covertly, like i said, we look. not because we want to
do anything with IT, with the unit. we don't. our competitive
instinct is at work here. we compare size, shape, color, gross-
ness, pubes, heft, etc. like Bowie says: 'boys check each other
out.' from grade school to the Senate floor they want to know
what you've got, or they want you to know what they've got.
so they look. you look. c'mon. in the high school locker room
when everybody was scared shitless about being found out,
everybody looked. not only that, if we don't look directly AT
it, we pick up on the choreography, the urinal dance. how it's
taken out and put it back in: a) camouflage your cock behind

hand or zipper and cut loose; b) stand back and fire into the hole, confident of your proud unit, certain of aim; c) be-stir the unbuckled belt, zipper, the opening of the slit in drawers, lowering of the drawers and engage in frenetic child-tear-ing-open-a-Christmas-present as prep for the spew. ditto the shake off: a) kill the thing and choke it to death; b) get rid of it quick and suffer a wet leg and spot; c) an in-between, half-hearted jerk, yellow drops on wrist and rub off on your pant leg. how did all these rules and behaviors get started, the ontological source of piss etiquette? i blame it all on Dad who lowered his flashlight with a fatherly slight-of-hand so that sonny boy could learn how to do it on his own. in silent instruction, Dad made it clear that one adheres to the rule of rules and does not look. ok? even as he checks out sonny boy's pencil as chip-off-the-old-block looks up at the old man's yard arm. Dad won't say it out loud—go ahead, boy, stare—but the rule and the breaking of the rule we probably got from Pop. that's what i think and so, when we walk back into the bar behind the stranger who minutes ago stood beside us shaking the be-jesus out of his thing, we know that he knows you saw it. or enough of it for both of you to think about it. one night i actually spoke up: 'dude, i gotta tell ya, ya got a gorgeous penis there.' that's right. i used the 'p' word. i thought 'cock,' but i said penis. i hate that word. whatever. i figured the kid would like to know that there was a queer out there who had sincere admiration for his gear. something to store away for future ref. 'wow. a dude liked my dick. i didn't let him suck me off or anything, but it was cool to get the props.' i realize

i took my life in my hands. that a forehead-to-stinky-urinal
might have been the bloody end game. but ya know what?
a life of caution ain't no life at all and rules are made to be
broken.

POOL HOPPING

beauty, we never forget it. the real-time imprint on the heart
of object, music, person is a Vasco da Gama love fountain. no
photograph or recording is as true or as affecting as the real
thing. it was all over Paris, the astonishing beauty of Pere
Lachaise, the Eiffel Tower at night, Notre Dame under 'clean
up' construction. when i heard Nina Simone throw back her
cowl at Woolsey Hall and open That Mouth to sing 'to be\
young, gifted and black.' beauty as a force of nature. it cracked
my chest open when we Whiffenpoofed for Pablo Casals in
Puerto Rico when i was drunk off my tits, his one diminu-
endo finger to his lips. i felt it watching Jack Kennedy deliver
his inaugural address on a black and white Motorola in the
driving snow. again when i saw the boy lift his head to smile
in the TV light in a warm living room in Moosup, CT. the
sight of a shining face, the shade of unfairly long lashes, the
hair on a wrist catching sunlight, a friend's eyes startled by
loss—all are are gifts from the human guru. i think in the
promised slow-motion reel we unspool in that split second
before death, we catch these rare remembrances across the

soul's silver screen. we were in love. we were drunk, sloppy and happy on the high cumulus of romance. 'ever go pool hopping?' he asked. 'nope.' 'we're going.' it's past midnight, stars diamond the sky. 'here's the deal. we find a mansion. we park. we look for a swimming pool. we crawl in on elbows and knees. we take off our clothes and slip into the water like alligators. we swim, we get out, we drag back on our gear and run barefoot across the sprinkling lawn.' the thought of seeing him naked in moonlight, mercury silver wet, smiling that smile of his, pumped blood a thousand-miles-per-second through my heart. 'sure.' so we did it. we found a house. we parked. we crept. dogs barked. we stripped (hadn't the time to worry about shriveled dick in cold air). we slithered across the flagstone and into the shimmering electric blue. the water was ice cold but the exhilaration of what we were doing, the fact that we were doing it together, the air, the light, the hush of whispers and the ecstasy in our eyes was mad mad beauty. he looked like a boy i'd met in a dream, or the boy kissing his lover in marble at the Louvre, or all the boys i'd ever loved in one face. his eyelashes were heavy, splayed wet, a suppressed laugh moved his belly, his sex just above the water line. that was the first time i saw him nude. things got complicated down the road, but that moment survived like a stolen portrait in the love attic. Keats got it right: beauty is truth.

THE SWITCH

romantic love: is it for-real possible without devolving into
George and Martha, into the black rain of the operatic? each
of us has our own Blue Valentine to lament or extoll. our
thumbs are up for the heart-wide-open, plug-into-socket
split-second when ego takes a back seat and the heart is the
driver. it's thumbs down when Mr. thrill-is-gone sticks his
tongue out and the ego re-takes the tiller. in my case the twist
in the wind begins as soon as i microscope the cold distance
infecting myself and the one i wake up thinking about. when
we start not saying the unsaid. when we resist the homework
required to love the one you're with. romance is a snap when
the connection can't wear thin from overuse, when a one-
night-only pair of eyes peers over a pint in me-too commiser-
ation or when a boy on a bus is a winner for the short ride. i
sat next to a kid on the way to New York City. i hung back in
the boarding line to snag someone who wouldn't stink me out.
my not-so-innocent 'would it be ok, ya know, if i sat here with
you?' worked. he was cool with it. a Brit, a musician, handsome and a talker. the time flew. we were castaways for the
afternoon. we never saw each other again, although he looked
me up online and we write. on the sad side lurks the decay-
ing relationship. the lying, the cover-up, the flayed flounder
that rots in the gut, entombing intimacy, spoiling the spark
that jump-started two lovers when both felt 'new.' a friend

suggested that in those first minutes we define the scope and
rules of the 'contract' to follow. for good or ill. eyes wander
over a hugged shoulder and lust for another. our ears pretend
to listen as we rehearse our next monlogue. judgement looks
over a book at a phony laugh. these are the petty annoyances
that sprout like scabies after a one-night stand. i'm guilty
on all counts. i've cheated in one way or another with just
about every person i've spent a decent number of days with.
i've pretended my beloved was a fascinating conversationalist
when all i was thinking about was what i wasn't getting done
while i was stuck there listening to him. i've choked back com-
ments about a body part that weirded me out (all are petty
crimes on the emotional docket). there are exceptions. there
always are. the primary love in my life grew like a pot plant
in the manure of my longest long-term relationship. he was
young, 20 years less than i, who magically, immediately, knew
my heart, my brain, my paranoid imaginings like a Gypsy
reading a palm. he knew when i was falling backwards into
doubt. he would catch and pull me back with a single look. he
knew who i was in all those places i feared uncovering after
our best-foot-forward honeymoon. the ones i'd eke out like
mustard gas to warn him off, to prove my unworthiness, to
be forgiven. you like me this much? ok, see if you can cope
with these worms in this head. it was a psycho test i could not
help running. we both did it, daring the other to challenge
the truth about who we were, of who we became and how we
created each other, wanting to earn our romantic diploma.
we wanted to be ever safe on the high bed of the heart, to

rock the universe, to carry the gleaming sword-in-stone' (the
show-off vanity of having scored a ten in loveland). i quit my
job as a cabbie and worked where he worked, where i'd met
him and where we happened, evolving a language of you-had-
to-be-there rituals that turned up the heat on a daily basis.
he'd climb up to my third-floor porch when my boyfriend
was out, heart like a cap-in-hand. we'd buy 40's and walk
the Arboretum, laughing, lost in the autumn light. we'd lie
under trees on damp leaves and do things he'd never thought
of doing but did for the love of me, urgently, awkwardly.
the pop song wonders, we did not. we had it all. and he was
beautiful to look at. all of him. i could watch his face for hours,
the shades of feeling as they moved over him like a dervish
spinning across a still pond. it was the luckiest time in my
life. i wrote a song about us, Over the Hill. WBCN played it
for weeks in summer drive time. he'd listen incognito, in a car
with friends who hadn't a clue. no one did. we were cloaked,
safe, in Neverland and now, because of him i no longer bin-
ocular the horizon for The One. i have no need, no desire to
find someone like him again even though all interactions vary
and who knows what lies dream-sleeping ahead in the road.
still, after all this, we ended badly. he was leaving for college.
long distance would make it difficult. we got stinking drunk
on what would be his last night home. we wept the hard, ugly
sobbing that accompanies loss. we walked around the block
and stopped, facing each other, wet with slobber and tears
and that's when it happened. that's when the switch moved
from on to off, the switch in my heart. i can't give a reason. i

still don't understand it. i'm not proud of it. a vortex of light, of energy shot up, out of the top of my being into the starry night. i became in that instant, neutral, emotionally flat-lined. i didn't love him anymore. not in that way. not in the way we'd been. it was so sad. i didn't say a word to him about it. i couldn't. in the next several years he sacrificed a lot to re-connect with me, a selfless boy, a generous man. but i was not there for him in my heart and i hurt him i'm sure, because he knew, of course he knew and forgave me as he always did, silently, spiritually. he's married now. he has two beautiful kids. he lives far from here. but i'd say, after all this time, that i can, in a blink, re-enter that Eden of the heart and see his eyes upon me, filled to the brim.

ASS

because you sit on it for hours, it is rarely clean or smooth or pretty. ass topography is speckled with pimply red bed-bug like dots and cuneiform hairs. a hammock of water-balloon flesh hides the under-ass parenthesis and worse, a shit chunk can get caught in ass hair and dangle like a tick in the jungle. a pristine, shiny, clear-skinned tight ass is a rare find indeed. it doesn't survive much past 14 which is why, after a few beers, a martini or a weed hit blurs your vision and makes it right, you ignore the spots, the dingle berry, the saggity ass and give it a squeeze or a bite. as for your very own back porch,

it is next to impossible to take in. a twist in front of a mirror
can offer a 3/4 snapshot but gives no indication of how broad
of beam or distended one has become. the stand-above-the-
mirror-on-the-floor approach reflects an alien ass crack high
on spider legs, walnut balls with a cock tip in a peek-a-boo,
sweaty bush. without a friend with a camera you'll never see
your fat ass the way it really looks. a friend of mine twirling
out of the shower felt a soft slap on the back of her upper thigh
only to realize that it was delivered by her very own cheek, a
blubbery wet buss. it made her laugh, but she was horrified.
i think asses begin, unless belonging to an athlete or a ballet
dancer, to find gravity in the late twenties and even if it's a
tight ass, it can become a dirty ass. it's been sitting on itself
long enough to accumulate a collection of creases and black
heads. if you're lucky your boyfriend or girlfriend will pop
and scrub and smooth you out like a soap stone. but the thing
is, no matter how disturbing this part of the body might be,
we're interested. we have to look. maybe face first, or tits, or
crotch, but a nice shot of a nice ass in blue jeans will not be
ignored. a kid walks by on the sidewalk and you turn and
you look. you always will. the way an ass walks is an action
miracle. male or female. a big hefty left, right, left ass-in-a-
dress is a Fellini spectacle worshiped for centuries. how many
tourists walk all the way around the Statue of David just to
catch a glimpse of that famous forever young rear end? maybe,
unless you're a total pedophile, a dirty ass, a be-zitted butt, an
ass crack with pubic seaweed sprouting out like a song, is hot
as hell. we all have our favorites. we all fantasize about how so

and so's will look out of shorts or stepping out of the shower.
we can't help it. we even watch each other watching. it gives
us a snort. and there are some asses impossible to picture. on
some, there's no movement whatsoever, or what appears to
be no ass at all, just a plumb line from the upper back to legs,
or, weirdly, an indentation, as if there's a vacant lot where on
others an actual ass bounces along with a smile. i would kill
to examine, like an archeologist, one of these ass negatives in
the flesh.

FALSE ENDINGS

'how can a thing so perfectly ended, continue?' is what Peter
Barrett said in a spoken word intro to 'Love Is Not Enough,'
the Orchestra Luna song that made it onto the 1974 record
(Epic). Peter complained: 'the Beatles say All You Need Is
Love and you're telling me Love Is Not Enough? i don't get
it.' i was thinking Bergman, not Lennon as in Through a
Glass Darkly. a boy's sister is insane. 'why can't she get better,
Father, when all of us love her so much? when she is surrounded by our love?' but it was not enough. she was helicop-
tered to an asylum. still, Peter had a point. how can an ending
continue? we get fed up, wrung out and quit on each other, on
a job, on family, on ourselves. all the love in the world, prior
to dissolution, fails until something unexpected happens. the
pencil flips (eraser to lead) and scratches a new sketch. jump-

ing out of a canoe in one direction sends it off in another. the
caterpillar becomes a butterfly. nevertheless, when doors close
we have a hard time imagining escape. it is not until we give
up completely that we can be born anew, or so the cliché spins.
and what about lovers who've thrown in the sweaty towel?
'she doesn't love me anymore. i can't take it. it's killing me!
i'm fuckin' outta here!' cries the losing boy. 'he's a douchebag.
he's checking out my best friend. he's always 'confiding' in my
fucking sister! i'm gonna throw up!' that's when the 'maybe we
can still be friends' coin hops into the fountain and bubbles
hope to the surface. 'i still love you. differently, ok? but we
understand each other too well to cast the baby out with the
bath water. maybe there's a new way to be.' so whispers the
cross-my-heart prayer. it is most often put forth by the losing
half and seems unrealistic to the one who cares less. and it's a
ploy to wrestle lost love back onto the sheets. 'we'll talk. have
coffee. learn to deal with the new person, ok?' is the argument
put forth to re-discover what had joined the two together in
the first place. the big unsaid: 'we're not fucking right now but
maybe we will again.' it's the fucking, isn't it, the sex. where
did the attraction go? why did it stop? who were you thinking about when i wasn't around? who were you fantasizing
when we were still together? who is sucking your cock, eating
you out, driving you crazy with impossible pleasure? sexual
jealousy, more than its emotional cousin, voids the 'let's be
friends' fantasy. unless one is, at long last, emotionally neutral or has that rare disinclination to be jealous, the ending is
true and not false. it's over. let it go. let him go. let her jump

out of the car and die. get over yourself. i love false endings in music, getting fooled into thinking that the song is over and then it's not. it's easier in art. to finish something only to fire it up again. to paint over a ruined canvas or wad up a waste-basket poem and try again. in love—not so simple. all those painful complicating failures and soul-lacerating endings, all the refused-to-be-believed expiration dates scream back at us from the chasm when love is not enough.

PLUM BOY

eating another diarrhetic breakfast on a quiet Sunday i see him with his friends. he's a geek. they're all geeks at his table. geeks are hot. i think they really put out in bed, even if there's stinky fingerpaint in unwashed tighty-whities or so i imagine. but there he is. knobby El Greco fingers pull-ing on chin hairs, picking his nose and rubbing his neck. he has enormous teeth, too many it seems, deep water blue eyes and a big jumpy smile. i can't tell about the hair. it's combed aggressively forward. when i get up to take a caffeine dump i pass by and glance at the crown. hmm, maybe he has an early spot? oh well, he's still hot, fuck it. then it begins. the looks above my book. he doesn't notice at first but like radar (i hate the tag 'gay-dar') he sniffs something in the air, eyes catch eyes and there's a bewildering fog in his Sinatra blues. he's not sure. was Freddie Krueger in the corner actually staring at him? he steals another glance and sure enough he knows. the book dude is in fact looking directly at his face and smiling as if to say 'hey, it's cool, just looking. you're cute. i like the sound of your laugh.' he blushes but quickly returns to his gesticulating conversation with fellow geeks. uh oh, something weird. he pushes his tongue out of his mouth in a chub arc, locking the tip behind his lower front teeth. his lips open and the tongue protrudes. it's as if he's sucking on a plum. a dark crimson orb when in fact it is his own engorged member. i don't think he knows what he's doing. maybe his friends are used to it or don't notice. who cares? i can't help staring. he's sexy even with the tongue trick and his leg, his right leg, is bouncing under the table like a jack hammer. i think he'd have fun over at my place for a visit. he'd let me look at him for longer periods of un-embarrassed time. of course i wonder if all these at-the-moment idiosyncrasies would, after awhile, turn me off and if i'd wind up hurting his feelings, build up his nascent narcissism only to tear it down. i remember years back another kid, a bad-breathed, yellow-toothed geek stayed the night. he wanted to. i doubt he'd done anything like that before, or would again. but somehow his awkward, skinny body fell into my bed. he might have left before dawn not wanting to be caught by roommates. i can't remember. but i would have loved to have been with the plum kid. at least i think i would. perhaps, like so many fantasies, it's best to have remained un-acted upon.

THE ROOF

may be the only place you can find infinity in a city—the big dome sky, clay-soft tar under bare feet, vertiginous ledge to piss over, a blimp lit from within circling Fenway like an overweight duck. i don't go up there often, but when i do it's with just one person and the time spent is as rare as the location. stars shoot, traffic below purrs like surf, moonlight quicksilver melts on the face of a boy, laughter lifts like beating wings, like a beating heart and closeness is possible and real. one night, up there, after wine and too many cheap beers, the two of us peek through splayed fingers at a fatty in his underwear bucking towards his girl in mock sex-god pantomime. he looks silly and doesn't know we're watching. we try not to be voyeurs but can't help it. we fall down on our backs giggling like naughty boys. we can't believe what we're seeing and the party in the next-door flat, raising bottles to us, has no clue. we move about, changing position, place and view. the conversation is wild and out of range, an acid escalator to the shifting pale pink clouds overhead. things are told that until this night were secret. these are dark, embarrassed, wonderful, poetic, sexy blood brother confessions. the waterspout we grab onto, like a rope on a keening ship, keeps us from falling into the bushes below when we piss, studiously apart from one another. a golden arc splashes onto the cement, chasing a cat and turns on lights that are movement activated. we hear Hispanic, stac-

cato cha-cha and buzz on a nearby porch, the girls invisible
and big-titted in our comic-book fantasy. we lie at the edge
above the street and spit. a white cotton ball floats haphaz-
ardly three stories to the sidewalk. in a laughing fit you stomp
on the tar and wake the guy in the bedroom below who didn't
want to be an asshole and make us shut up. we imagine he
might send up to our roof in his place a magic girl, a proxy,
to tell us that although she's fine with the noise, he isn't. she
will hug you and touch your face as if fireflies had landed on
your cheek. she will leave with a silent Navaho drift, her skirt
like soft breath and vanish downstairs and we are alone again.
we are close up here, you and i, as if proximity isn't possible
in other places. statements pontificate and play, but it's ok. we
know how silly and how deep we talk. time stops or flies as
we ride the wave. the imagined glint of sunrise soon to flash
on the curve of earth tells us it's late and time to go. we are
lucky for the hours we had, uninterrupted. sex has happened
here and kissing, but not with you. love and sex hover like
hornets but do not bite. we are probably thinking about it,
me more than you and you not with me but the sex talk is
honest, hot, revelatory and brave. it is as if we could, but can't
or won't. there's been five nights of this. one would have been
enough, i guess, but we go for repeats. it is astonishing and
ridiculous that it has worked more than once. when something
so wonderful happens we worry we'll mess it up with repetition, but fuck it, worry never got anyone anywhere. you say:
'language is the biggest obstacle to communication.' i say: 'my
heart cracks open when you're around.' 'yes,' you reply, men-

tioning Joyce whom i cannot read. maybe you will read him to me aloud some night on this roof. we thump downstairs into a dark kitchen, down a dark hallway, outside onto the sidewalk we just looked down upon. we shiver and i walk you home, off-roof. we finger snap 'good-night' with exhausted smiles. the sky is more full with fading stars and a thin pale moon.

MIKE'S PRAYER

i let Mike drive Michelle's VW all over the the Vineyard. we drove to Jungle Beach, through an opened gate and right up the path. we ran to the edge of the cliff and plunged down the slope, wind in our ears, tears stinging our eyes. we stopped at the hard flat beach, out of breath. staring at each other. we went back up to the car. Mike was driving like a crazy man. on the wrong side of the road, up on banked curves, too fast. i was trying to make him see that he needed to be responsible, that he should respect property that doesn't belong to him (fat chance). finally, i got him to pull over. i sat in the passenger seat in stony silence. Mike lit a cigarette. 'i bet you wish we were back in Boston and i was back in Reddington Pond (a group home for delinquent kids in Maine). you don't want to be with me at all…huh.' silence. 'you really don't want to be with me at all, right? you can say.' i was observing the manic rise and fall of my impatience. i was trying to act calm but i felt lousy and it was written all over my face. i needed to meditate. it was late afternoon. the sun was beating down in sharp golden angles in the trees. Mike spotted a soft field off to the right and drove right into it, parking on the crest of a hill, facing the sun. i shut my eyes and started the mantra in my head. Mike popped a pistachio nut with his front teeth. he lit up a Marlboro. he turned the starter on and off. 'Mike...' 'what's wrong? you getting mad?' one definitive nod. 'okay. i'll go for a walk.' when i came out of it the sun was grazing the treetops, splintering light in all directions. Mike was nowhere to be seen. i heard an unearthly primitive singing, far away. i got out and called for him. no reply. it was getting colder and darker. i drove around the field. in the distance a dot of red flannel, arms outstretched, odd bundles of branches, like sage, in each fist. blinding grin. he looked at me half-crazed. 'where have you been, Mike? what have you been doing?' 'praying.'

GIVING UP ON 'GOD'

how do these things happen? the moment we fall (or rise) in love? i don't think it's ever said—not right off. those three words. maybe they aren't even in your head. your knees give out in spite of yourself. in spite of all expectation, self-protection, longing. but there it is. that incredible bullet in the heart. and it can happen late, really late, in life. and it can happen early. Tommy never knew i fell in love with him. i don't think i ever put it that way even to myself. i was 14 i think, or maybe a year older. and i wasn't the only one. many of us at school had that stab in the gut over this kid. the sun stood behind him wherever he was. blazing smile, boy's regular haircut, sport-ready arms and legs. i was a year or two older. he wasn't in my class. he would visit my friends next door because he was their age. i hung on the periphery. all my get-into-trouble adolescent skills stuttered around him. i felt lucky just to be near that golden energy. when i think about him now i recall Martha (Who's Afraid of Virginia Woolf?) describing her fantasy son whose 'hair was blond before all the other boys.' that rarified over-the-top memory. i'm not even sure Tommy and i ever spoke about anything that mattered. i just wanted always always to be near him whenever i could. the odd thing was, he had an allergy. he could not be stung by a wasp and survive. this was before there was the emergency shot to fix it. and so it happened. he got stung. he died, 12 or 13 years old. everyone went crazy. school stopped classes to pray for him. our little group on Atlee Rd. stayed home. we walked silently to an old stone Episcopal church to pray for him. pray that he'd come back. if there was a God, we figured, He would save someone as beautiful as Tommy. there was no resurrection. we gave up on God that day. God failed us. He failed Tommy. strange thing is, i still love him. i still 'see' him in my heart. the sun still leaps out of his smile. the infinity of the soul is known to me through this boy i could only be close to without ever really knowing if i was.

WORSHIPING WARREN

i used to sit in Warren's room at Saybrook College (Yale), a
fire in the fireplace. we would drink and drink and drink. he
was a sort-of rock star there. i worshipped him, his beautiful,
soaring, evocative singing voice—tenor, his depth of culture.
we talked late into the night. he had carved 'Excalibur' on
the wrist of the armchair i always sat in (not sure why, didn't
ask). he and his girlfriend, Micaela, a total knockout, would
listen to that slow, agonizing 'Death Und Libestod' section
of Tristan and make love to it, trying to have mutual orgasm
at its peak. 'we always missed,' he laughed. 'we were always
early.' he majored in Chinese studies and quickly mastered the
language. he got me into the Whiffenpoofs. he got me into
Wolf's Head (a secret society). he got me through my first
year at Yale by seeming to believe in me, or perhaps enjoying
my belief in him. i looked up to him, but was never in love,
beautiful as he was bearing a close resemblance to Dylan
in his early years, same wild hair, intense eyes. years later i
ran into someone in New York when we were recording the
Orchestra Luna record. someone who knew Warren. he told
me where to look him up. i went the next day, full of anticipa-
tion. his place was a walk-up on a tiny street in the village. i
pushed a greasy ivory nipple buzzer. 'who is it?' 'it's me, Rick.'
he met me at the door, unshaven and smelling of booze. he
hugged me, kissed me. our lips missed. unwashed dishes were
piled in the sink. dirty clothes and newspapers were all over

the place. tapes and ashtrays full of butts. says he's giving up smoking but rips into one after another. vodka and orange juice in a coffee cup. tells me about a famous vocal coach named Richard, an old man in his sixties. an ex-baritone with a huge rich voice. Warren played me the tapes. this guy had loved Warren, believed in his talent. all this took place in San Francisco. Warren had studied with him for a year when the old man suddenly died. it broke his heart. broke his spirit and his drive. he moved to New York to study law and to continue voice with one of his mentor's students. he clutched at a broken pitch pipe. he would bleat out a note and attempt in a smeary drunken pathetic way to sing, one aria after another, with his marble eyes fixed on me. 'tell me, Rick. do you notice the difference? how much freer the voice is?' 'yes,' i lied. so sad and deluded. his voice was awful. his phrasing off. no life in it, only struggle. there was one note in particular that was giving him a hard time. he kept going back to it. 'here,' he said, blowing on the pitch pipe, 'i'll try again. no. don't go. i won't sing anymore. stay for dinner, Rick. please stay. you are the only person from Yale...' 'no, i can't. i really can't. too much to do. i'll call.' 'no, you must stay longer. can't you stay?' he threw his arms around me. his breath was nasty, his desperation. all the miserable alcoholic phony emotional bullshit that i used to get from Dad and between me and whomever i was enthralled with at the time. love like days of wine and roses. but he repulsed me. i stood very still. 'Warren. i really think you should give up the booze. it can't be good for your voice. at any rate, i'll call.' what an asshole i was. i prayed for him in my facile may-the-force-be-with-you, gauzy-hippie, wishy-washy way but kept a safe distance. he hugged me pretty hard, pressed his cock into me. i froze. i walked out.

¶

ANIMAL KINGDOM

"No matter how much cats fight, there always seem to be plenty of kittens."
— *Abe Lincoln*

"We are Siamese if you please. We are Siamese if you don't please."
— *The Lady and the Tramp (Disney)*

THE REAL THING

we had a silver-blue Weimaraner named Boo (after Boo
Radley). he had yellow eyes and a sweet disposition, which
was unusual for his breed. most of the Weimeraners i'd met
were high-strung, bug-eyed and scrawny. Boo was on the
mournful side. maybe because we had his balls cut off—what
was left was an embarrassing prune that everyone could see
under his clipped tail—and he hated being observed while
doing his business. he'd crane his neck around in the squat
position to see if we were watching. 'go away' he seemed to be
saying under concerned eyebrows. he also had a serious fart
problem. they would hiss out of his ass like a steam iron and
he'd look more world-weary than ever, staring at his behind
with an oh-God-what-WAS-that?! expression, then he'd rise
and lope to another room, repulsed by his own stench. as a kid
i remember they would issue forth under the card table where
my Grandmother played bridge with her friends. tap, tap,
tap she'd drum her forefinger waiting to snap down a card.
Boo would erupt, get up and leave the room, the left-behind
odor so overwhelming it seemed to 'appear' under the table,
wafting up into the nostrils of Granny and co. Granny was a
Yankee stalwart with a no-nonsense reaction: a single raised
eyebrow. Boo's best friend in the world was a neighborhood
Dachshund named Mopsy who was as diminutive and ladylike
as Boo was substantial. copper brown with tiny sharp teeth
and clickity-clackity toe nails, she lived down the hill, across

a skirt of lawn, over a stream and up a slope in a big, brand-
new, millionaire's, mustard-stucco mansion. every now and
then she'd wander on to our field—a nearly-invisible spot
against the grass. one afternoon, when my dad and his pals
were driving golf balls off an imaginary tee near our house,
one of the balls hit her in the ribs. she blew up like a balloon,
small black eyes in the middle of a basketball (she had a habit
of getting in the way). one time i was painting a four-by-eight
foot Picasso rip-off for an art show at high school. it had to be
laid on the floor for me to work on it. Mopsy castanetted her
sharp black nails across the painting, i suppose in an effort
to satisfy her curiosity. or, just to fuck with me. the paints—
made from egg whites (the fresco materials were a mix of pig-
ment powder and egg) —weren't yet dry when Mopsy added
her 'art' to the project. i picked her up by the skin on her back
and heaved her across the room and out the door. i didn't feel
good about it but Mopsy didn't need human love, she had Boo
who visited her every day. Boo befriended Charlie, the milk-
man, who'd toss him a milk bone, let him hop into the truck
and drove him down to the Mopsy Mansion. there, Boo and
Mopsy would hang out, go on a garbage hunt, get their fill
and walk back up the slope to our house where they'd sit, side-
by-side, just off the flagstone porch and stare down the hill
like a couple of old ladies in rockers. to us they were romantic
lovers. when it was time for Mopsy to head home, Boo'd walk
her the whole way down. he was dark after she died (at 17) and
never the same. left, himself, not long after.

MOUSE TWITCHING

my cat, Sofi Wan Kenobi (or Sofia Di Putzi, or Sofi Anon
depending on my mood) is a runt with a tiny head and a tiny
body. she has a funny, off-kilter walk and a lopsided, skit-
tering run. in fact, she gallops (i hear there's a ten-syllable
German word for this) up and down the hallway of our apartment—thundering 'hoofs.' i chase her in my socks, trying
to imitate her, to make her run faster. she loves this. Sofi is
inky black with yellow/green eyes and a few straggly, white
hairs on her chest. she distrusts everybody: she hid behind a
couch for two weeks when i got her, used, from a girl moving to the West Coast. the girl called her Zoey, which was
cool but i had to name her for myself. if i was gonna feed her
and solicit her affection, then i should call her what i wanted.
strangely, she's a one-man cat and i'm her man. he who feeds
her... but of course there's more to it than that. i think she got
kicked around in her old neighborhood, like Nixon, and it's
still with her, the paranoia. she's also sweet. when she watches
TV in my lap, her purr is so loud you can hear it in the next
room. she licks my hands and arms to wake me up in the
morning and she's a pro at those seductive i-love-you eyes.
last summer i had to have a few of her teeth extracted. they
were rotten at the root. it cost a small fortune. she survived
the surgery, but had to be fed mushed-up tuna and water
for weeks, hating the dry pellets when forced to go back. an
embarrassing result—her tongue gets caught in the space of

her missing tooth during a licking session, it gags her and
she reels it back in her tiny throat like a curly, birthday horn
contracting—tourettes kitty. i refuse to let her get fat. i'm
obsessive about it. 'too much to ask of a dime-sized heart,' i
rant. i feed her parsimonious portions four times a day which
means she wakes me up at 6:30 in the morning, staring at
me. 'NO,' i say. 'NO, SOFI!' but she's right. she's always right
about feeding time. i lumber out of bed, feet like ski boots and
clink her pellets into the bowl. afterwards i can't sleep. i read.
noir fiction while my noir cat glares, nose-to-nose, hoping
for a post-breakfast scratch. i give in, pat, purr, scratch, lean,
purr, read. she's a hunter. handling the mice problem is sport.
i can tell she's caught one when i hear her leap up and through
the secret door in my closet making muffled 'roar' sounds,
mouse in mouth. she lets it go, chasing it to bits until death.
i find the shriveled creature in the morning, tweeze its tail
with a square of toilet paper and dump it in the toilet. when
she doesn't kill it dead and it's not alive enough to interest her,
it twitches on the floor, tiny feet just so. i touch the tail and
one little matchstick leg shivers. i jump, horrified. i can't put it
in the garbage until i'm sure it's totally utterly kaput. i won't
let it suffocate in the stench. but it hurts, this Mother Nature
struggle, which Sofi always, always wins. i'm proud of her but
i feel bad for da poor, widdle mousey.

MOUSE EVEREST

wrapping the day up with late night emails i sense movement overhead—a scratching and a struggle. i look up and—i
swear to God—there's a mouse climbing the window curtain, way-the-fuck up there, near the ceiling, scrambling his
skittery cuteness along the edge and vanishing on the upper
ledge. how does he do it, clutch curly-fry toenails? and where
is Sofi? 'sick em, Sof!' i yell, 'get that motherfucker!' which is
two-faced for me who always feels Dali Lama-sorry for the
hard-as-a-rock dead thing left by my cat after she's finished
him off, no longer a toy to bat around. God knows where the
thing went or if it is even actually up there but it gives me the
shivers. the fat lady with the rolled knee stockings is high on
a chair, skirt in fist, faint from the sight of the little bugger.

PUT TO SLEEP

—the euphemism. of course there's nothing sleepy about it.
it's a white-lie murder. when i was a kid we put dogs down, a
lot of them, for doing bad things: for killing sheep, for chasing
a child around the block, for being old. 'the Kinscherfs
always kill their dogs,' said a friend. what we did not do was
be there when it happened. we drove, crying, with the dog in
the back seat unaware of his fate. just another ride in the car.
we huddled, terrified, in the waiting room while Boo or

Caesar or Fawny got euthanized. animals live in the guru
present, right? if pain is what they have, so be it. but do their
doggy brains wonder about the end of everything? about
being put to sleep? i doubt it. but on a bus ride to New York
City i saw a dead dog on a cement island in the middle of the
highway, a hit and run. a revolving parade of dog pals, 20 or
30 strong, circled the body in the late afternoon remembering
their friend from woo-hoo haunts around town: the garbage
dumps they pigged out on, the flower beds they shat in, the
cats they treed. they came to say goodbye, to honor a fallen
comrade. but this is not a story about them, it's about Ralph,
my cat, a second-hander who poked his paw out of a cage in a
shelter in Philadelphia to touch my boyfriend's hand. 'this is
the guy,' he smiled. we were gonna give him to my Mom who
had only weeks before put Sydney, her overweight longhair,
to sleep but she didn't want our guy. she didn't want to suffer
another gruesome loss. the vets in Philly decided that we'd
make good parents so they spent their money to fly Ralph up
to Boston. we met him at airport, drove to Jamaica Plain and
cut him loose in the apartment. it turned out he hated us on
sight. the paw through the cage was a ruse. we told him he
had 48 hours to chill or we'd send him back to Philly or put
him down and that's when i prayed, a fool's mumbo-jumbo
involving light with a capital 'L,' The Force and a mental
picture of Mickey, the cat we'd had on life support at an all-
dyke animal hospital, until, as they say in the obits, 'following
a long battle with cancer' she was, you got it, put to sleep. i
prayed to Mickey to fix Ralph, to correct his character and

turn him into a cool cat and oh my god, in seconds, i swear, he shape-shifted into a fabulous kitty-witty. a smarty-pants who could jump from floor to bureau, poke at a quarter, a watch, a picture frame until it clattered to the floor and woke us up, who could climb a drain pipe from yard to second story, tip-toe the gutter and scratch at the screen until we let him in. and he was funny. he corrugated his whiskers into a TV antennae by sunning under a 150-watt lamp. he snuck into the fridge and choked on a turkey carcass until we found him in the cold, shivering his face off. he had those i-love-you-but-watch-it eyes that owned your heart and he stayed healthy until he hit 17. that's when he got it, the cat curse, kidney damage. we infused him with fluid from a saline sack hung from a coat hanger. he hated it. he hated being caught under the bed, wrapped in a straight-jacket towel, crushed on the kitchen table and jabbed in his lower neck. when it was over he looked like he'd sprouted a fanny pack of fur Jello. the infusions added a couple of years, same as chemo provides a cancer patient temporary remission, but doesn't save a life. Ralphie slowed down. he couldn't leap onto the bed, let alone floor to bureau and he got the shits. black goo squirted out of his ass as he dragged it across the rug, a Jackson Pollack of hot tar in his wake. the stench was unimaginable. we had to put our dear Ralphie to sleep. but this time it would be different. this time we would face reality head on. we would not hide outside the execution room. we would suffer, like Truman Capote watching Perry Smith hang from the neck until dead, we would suffer the truth of the euphemism.

Ralphie was not being put to sleep, he was being put to death.
the vet was a large lady with a nice face who assured us a) we
were doing the right thing because Ralphie's quality of life
was nil and b) that it wouldn't hurt. the room was small with
a shiny metal table, a basin and a bright, overhead neon tube.
we nuzzled his neck while the doc filled the syringe and stuck
it into the exact spot where we'd prolonged his life. his mouth
was a silent shriek, his eyes narrowed and his back arched in
a grotesque reverse curve until he collapsed, asleep forever.
it did not look painless. no, sir. it looked like it hurt a lot. we
found out later that the proper method includes not one but
two injections: one to induce sleep, another to kill. we were so
out of our minds viewing the spectacle we couldn't remember
if he'd been given one or two. it sure looked like he hadn't. it
looked to us like he went through hell. they stuck his ashes in
a Styrofoam box—a hamburger put to sleep.

KITTY PROJECTION

(FOR SOFI WHO'S NO LONGER OF THIS EARTH)

my cat is neurotic. she will not to be picked up unless the pellets are about to hit the bowl and then just behind her shoulders, legs stiff as drum sticks, a measly 3, 4 feet off the lino-

leum and not in arms, not hugged against chest. visitors 'oo'
and 'ah' and reach out to pet her but she flits away, fussy and
paranoid. with visitors she hides in my closet on a shelf waiting impatiently for them to leave. if a dog barks she hibernates
until it's gone. on the other hand, with me, she's awesome. she
sleeps under the covers, in the crook of my arm, on her back,
purring. she loves to have her belly rubbed when it's cold out.
her prized trick is to slip in and out of my bedroom through a
pantry portal between the kitchen and my room, a miniature
swiss window she discovered when we moved in 10 years ago.
she's getting on, 10-12 years old. i worry that once she hits
17 she'll be shitting herself and unable to jump, to access the
glory hole. when she arrived at my apartment for the first
time she hid behind a couch for two weeks until she got up the
tits to emerge and stake out the territory. for years that territory has been this apartment, unshared with any other beast.
a revolving door of roommates and friends until last week
when a new kitty, an irresistibly-cute, fluffy, Yoda-whiskered
guy moved in, skin, bones and fur. his name is Mao after the
Chinese dictator. my roommate thought he looked dictatorial
with his tough-guy stance and big paws. we went down the
list—Hitler, Stalin, Idi, Pol Pot—and chose Mao, because, ok,
that's the sound he makes: 'mao.' we love the little fella. how
could we not? he's irresistible. but Sofi is petrified. Mao scam-
pers about the house on curiosity skates and Sofi hides on her
shelf like a rejected glove. i don't know what's going on in her
kitty brain, but i imagine all sorts of terrible thoughts: that

i'm cheating on her, that i don't love her anymore, even as i pat her more than ever. i've made my bedroom her sanctuary so she can eat in peace. once Mao's big enough to leap through the hole, that'll be the end of the quarantine. at first i blamed her. i thought, fuck, get over yourself, Sof, you weirdo. any other cat would have handled the kid no problem. but i call the vet and she tells me that this is normal. that it might take one to six months to a year for Sofi to adjust, if not longer. a friend of mine went through the same thing with her guy and that cat is still, two years down kitty lane, freaked. i did take one indulgent step: the vet suggested a product from France, a plug-in atomizer good for a month. it wafts oily feline fumes into the atmosphere that have a calming effect on an upset kitty. sometimes it works, sometimes not. but i bought the Eau de Chat and it seemed to do the job. Sofi acquired a sort of Xanax equilibrium. occasionally she peeks around the kitchen corner and stares down the hall at Mao who's staring back from the far end. maybe when no one's home they hang out and have a laugh over how worked up we humans get over all this. i love her. i need her to be ok. i tell her that. she purrs. i imagine she listens and is working on it with some invisible, screwball shrink. coda: things seem to be better of late. both creatures lie on the same bed blinking at each other, paws crossed.

NUREYEV REVIVES FONTEYN

he pulls her out of retirement. they dance on big stages across the globe. she's young again. he's leaping to inspired heights. they adore each other. the other night i'm watching the last five minutes of Toy Story 3 and working up a good cry when i notice my spinster cat, Sofi, on top of the foot stool. underneath is the new kid, Mao, who looks up at her with half-closed but curious golden eyes. Sofi half-heartedly paws the air with a matchstick leg. Mao seems half asleep, but they're communicating. what was once fight and scratch has for the moment become what i can only describe as play, or off-hand shadow boxing. Mao has drawn her outside her stay-in-the-safe-closet persona and now they're in kitty love. she prefers to leave my room when i go to sleep rather than crash at the foot of my bed. she wants to be out there in the hallway with Mao. they've slept body-to-body when i caught them in an unguarded moment and the other morning he stood watch at the door to the porch while she shat in her box, undisturbed, like the centurion boyfriend who guards the men's room while his girlfriend takes a hurry-up piss. it took months, this ever so gradual friendship and on Christmas day, i swear, as Sof was curled up on a couch pillow, Mao leaped up, clumsily tip-toed over to her and kissed her on her hard licorice-lipped kitty-mouth. a tiny cat-kiss like a bird fart. they still wrestle and scratch and bite and hiss and spit, but it's closer to a good time than a hate-fest. so on top of Toy Story 3 i get this image of two ex-enemies in a paw-de-deux.

HOW DO THEY KNOW?

dogs (and cats), when you're hurting? they do, don't they?
when i was a kid we had a Standard poodle (the only one of
the many dogs we had growing up that we disliked) who
looked after my granddad after he lost his wife. he slept in a
tiny room (the 'maid's room') at the end of a long hallway on
the second floor. the poodle would trot down the hall, sit at
the side of the bed and rest his chin on the mattress next to
Granddad, looking mournfully up at him with big brown eyes.
he knew. he gave solace in ways none of us could.

I SHIT YOU NOT

Sofi Wan Kenobi, in her declining years, pisses and shits in
weird places. places other than her glitzy shiny new black 'n
white 'BMW' litter box. i don't think she does it on purpose.
she's doing her elderly best. she can't strap on an old lady's
diaper. she can't telegraph her defecation location so i can
intervene. she's getting used to her new box, but accidents
happen. the other night i smelled cat shit at 4 am. it woke
me up. i thought no way. she couldn't. she wouldn't. maybe
it's one of her rare cat farts. maybe she shat in the kitchen
and it wafted into my bedroom. forget about it, Berlin. go
back to sleep. five minutes later the stench is still in the air.
i snort and sniff like Devine in Polyester. i yank on the lamp

149

light and there on my floor are three semi-hard Tootsie
Rolls, underbelly wet and curdling the room. Sofi is purring.
i scrape 'em up into a paper towel, jaw clenched, and squirt
chemicals at the spot in hopes that her remains won't invite a
recurrence. why is this happening!? in trying to leap through
the closet portal into the kitchen to take a proper dump in
the proper box, is she thwarted? are the jump-up level boxes
i setup to make it easy for her not properly aligned? does she
give up, have to go and do her business on my floor because
she can't help herself? is she vindictive? 'he didn't get things
right so i'm gonna shit on his fucking floor…' does her aging
sphincter fail to hold tight (and that's only the shit angle). the
piss part, that foul acidic toxin, permeates the apartment. it
hits you in the nose when you unlock the door and though it
does have a grapefruit-like altered state, it reeks. i've read that
this is not uncommon among grandma kitties, but it's nasty.
i can't tell where it's coming from: the bathroom? the living
room? the kitchen in front of the fridge? the back porch?
(sniff and search) case solved: one afternoon when i see her
crouched on the lower shelf of the plant table, belly to grid,
cutting loose onto the tile. splashy-splashy with a kitty face
warning: 'don't watch.' today, armed with the anti-cat piss
product, i wipe things down again, fingers crossed that she
will stop once and for all. i don't blame her—she's old—but
there have been times when she came after me on purpose: a
visitor was visiting (Sofi is not fond of shared affection). we
were getting it happening when that ungodly turd curtain hit
the bedroom air. there she was: on my bed, back arched with

black Team America turds curling out of her furry hole. the
kid bounced—abrupt end of visitor and visit. 'Sofi!!! for fuck's
sake!! this is over the line!!!' she didn't care. Sofi and Rick: a
dysfunctional love affair.

EXIT RAMP

the old girl is shifting rapidly into elderly gear: frail back end,
an awkward, embarrassing struggle to leap onto bed or couch,
long periods of rest under the radiator, in pain when i pet her,
kitty dementia that makes her hard of hearing and causing her
meows to be screams—a tiny lion in pain. no more galloping
down the hallway. she's 20. i've been telling friends for years
that she's 19, so i bumped it up to 20. that's a lot of human
years. her fur's still soft and kept clean but she eats next-to-
nothing and licks her hole more than usual. i took her to the
vet seven months ago with these symptoms. they gave her an
antibiotic shot and an appetite stimulant (liquid weed?). in two
days she was a teenager, her full, awesome self. but this week,
she hit the wall all over again. i took her back up. got the shot.
gave her the stimulant as a pill which, as predicted, made
her foam at the mouth like an epileptic. spewed white froth
all over her loathsome kitty suitcase. she hated it and contin-
ued to eat nothing at all. she's weak and slow. the meekest of
purrs. my poor girl. somehow, tradition still applies. when i'm
in bed she struggles up onto my chest, twists and turns and
settles down to sleep. makes me hope she's got many months

of life ahead. we pass out. around three AM there's an explosion: a burst of light, a miniature fireball arcing in front of my desk. i rub my eyes awake. what the fuck was that!? stench of electric burn in the air. i crack open the window and then i see it. sofi had pissed on the nest of electric chords and made a miniature yellow pond under and around the power strip. she could have been electrocuted! the reverse zing that happens when you try to light a fart and it goes 'back up.' what i think happened was that after she cut loose it took time to seep into the strip before it hit the explosive jackpot. thank god there wasn't a fire. this girl is going out with a bang.

GOING WITH THE FLO

Ed stuck his head out the front door to whistle for Flo (overweight black lab) to come home for dinner. nothing. he walked out to the middle of Ridgemont St. way down, a tiny black dot. 'Flo! FloooooOH!' the dot didn't move. Ed walked closer. Flo lay on her back, legs wide open, head completely lost inside a ripped-open hole in a black plastic garbage bag, garbage juice trickling down her neck. she was in ecstasy. 'FLO!' she flipped up and out like she'd been shot, landing on her feet, jiggling all over, apologizing and apologizing with those unmistakable 'i'm sorry' eyes. a scrap of tin foil was stuck in her mouth. she smelled like shit. i guess if my mother had ever caught me jerking off...

¶

NOT KIDDING

"We're not put here just to have a nice life."
— Baba Ram Dass

"Perhaps only people who are capable of real togetherness
have that look of being alone in the universe."
— D. H. Lawrence (Lady Chatterly's Lover)

TED

i had to go. i'd been to St. Patrick's as a teenager to honor
Bobby. going this time was just as critical. i dislike lines
and crowds. i went to the Sox victory parade in '04 and the
first one for the Pats in the snow. i was glad i went but after
waiting for hours on numb feet just to see the boats lumber
by i was let down, bored, wondering 'is that all there is to a
victory parade?' sure, it was good to plant my feet in honor
of the hard-earned, long-time-coming victory and to see
the rock-star athletes on display in real time. but once was
enough. on the other hand, i liked being in line to hear Obama
speak during the campaign. the people, thousands upon thousands, psyched, inspired, and happy to be a part of something
bigger than any routine, as if all of us were one. that was the
last time i saw Teddy. he was bellowing on stage to introduce
the new torchbearer. i'd also met him, years back, in a bar.
shook his generous hand, 'good ta meet ya, Senator...' etc. it
was not that big a deal but something never forgotten. on the
way to the JFK Library, on the T and looking out the window it seemed as if a lot of guys looked like him, overweight,
chin-up-jaunty, toothy grin, with eyes on the sky and feet on
the ground but they weren't the man. no one was or ever will
be. not in my lifetime. the line was as diverse racially as it
could be in this ol' whitey town. there were tears wiped away
under sunglasses, eyes downcast or uplifted or both and kind
thoughts about strangers. i was gonna read to pass the time in

the long line, but i didn't. i quietly inched towards the under-sail-like library with everybody else. the Kennedy kids were there, thanking us for coming, for showing up to honor their grandfather, for loving the world he believed could be better even as dark forces conspired against it. inside the Smith Hall, where I'd seen Paul Krugman speak, lay the great man in state, surrounded by soldiers who didn't blink, by members of families who'd lost love ones on 9/11, who'd been connected to the Senator in loss and by members of the Kennedy clan who sat quietly on spindly metal chairs. we had to be there, all of us, to honor this storm of a man who outlasted so many hurricanes in his personal and public life. we need him now more than ever. every time, every time i hear the words: 'and the dream shall never die' tears fill my eyes.

I WILL NEVER TRULY KNOW. EVER.

watching last weekend's Winter Soldier II (Iraq veterans against the war) i was struck by how distant i am from know-ing, in any profound or visceral way, what it is that a soldier, any soldier, suffers. i've not been there to watch my comrade get shot to death or have his arm blown off. i've not been there when the machine gun in my hand severs the head of the 'enemy' while his son looks on. i've not been there arriv-ing home, stepping off a bus, looking into the eyes of family,

friends, loved ones and feeling that they can never comprehend where i have been, what i have seen or what i have done.
i've not had my humanity trained out of me, dehumanizing
and demonizing 'the other.' i've never known the screaming
pain of having my leg exploded by a roadside bomb, my face
acned with shrapnel or my mind lost in the paranoid nightmare of PTSD. i never will unless Jamaica Plain is invaded
and i take up a butter knife to defend my old lady's railroad
apartment. i sit stunned in front of the computer screen as i
listen the story of the father who takes his 22-year-old son's
body into his arms and lifts him up out of the garden hose
noose he had used to hang himself. i collect with others in
the rain for an anti-war vigil by the JP Civil War Monument.
we are few. cars honk by in the drizzle. our quiet assemblage
is not noticed by anyone who has the power stop this war.
my 'out of Iraq, now' sign blurs in the wet and assuages no
one hurt or destroyed in battle. i fear this unknowing on my
part although i am grateful to have never known the hot hell
of war. i ache for those who cry out, but my pain is nothing
compared to theirs. i think, 'God bless, you' but i don't know
who or what God is.

DANCING WITH CUBA

i'm a busy guy. i like to think so. if i'm hurtling through the
day, the last thing i need is some unexpected distraction

or person obliterating my bullet-head, get-out-of-my-way
schedule. i slither out of most of them with a big laugh or a
joke at my expense but sometimes i can't get away with it. the
onslaught is too persistent or too cute to say no to. it's a good
thing too because those are the times it's a good idea for me
to fend off the ticker tape—the static in my head—and face
the unpredictable. about a week ago i dropped downstairs
to La Casa del Regalos where my landlady, the irrepressible
Aida, holds court and keeps my mail for me (i lost the key to
our mailbox a few months back). Aida retrieves it from the
mailman, straps on a rubber band to hold what is mostly junk
in place and points it out to me with her big, Cuban smile,
hands clasped together in front of her waist. last week she had
her blaster blasting serious Cha-Cha music. she twirled up at
me, grabbed my wrists and made me dance with her. laughing it up in her high soprano, musical laugh. dip, spin, twirl,
laugh, Cha Cha Cha. it was crazy. i was completely caught up
in it and i hate to dance. i'm the sour pus at the wedding when
all the drunks are up on the floor shimmying and grinding
and i feel like an idiot. i can't wait to get outta there. last time
i actually got off on dancing was on a hit of ecstacy at a gay
bar with a very cute 'straight' kid. we were not appreciated.
too many big gestures that didn't go with the territory. it
took a pill to get me out of myself enough to not think about
every little dumb move i was making and that was on one rare
night. dancing with Aida was another. i think the two events
are at least 15 years apart, but maybe, had i lived in Cuba...

IS THERE EVER ANOTHER PLACE TO BE OTHER THAN WHERE YOU ARE?

you're in a dungeon, strapped to a table with electric alligator teeth snapped onto your balls. a guy in an executioner's mask has his hand on the trigger and he ain't a dominatrix, he's a motherfucking sadist who will get you to say anything, do anything, fuck anything and you will not resist. if you could 'jump' to a safe harbor, you would, wouldn't you? i would. and so, isn't it true that we're always in the right place at the right time with the right situation or person? what i'm stabbing at here is the realization (increasingly as i get older) that all experience benefits The Self in spite of our too many all-too-human, grass-is-greener complaints. even when it seems the opposite. even when we wish to be almost any other place than right here, right now. 'you ok?' i ask the dishwasher. 'i just want to get the fuck outa here and go home.' but he can't, can he? he has to finish up or quit. that's how we learn. that's how we grow. the unavoidables that we resent and confront and grope our way past. a hairdresser friend of mine put it this way describing parents who hope to protect their kids from hurt and harm: 'we can't keep their lessons from them even if we wanted to.' case in point: i've been a waiter at the same joint for 29 years. my friends can't believe it. 'are you

kidding!? 29 years?!' or from a returnee: 'are you still here?'
is that running in place or is that running in place? whatever,
i love the job. i always have. i actually look forward to going
to work. the unpredictability of the customers, the absurd
soap-opera gossip employees whisper, the kids you watch, like
a high school teacher, grow up and fly the coop, irritated by
the parents they once revered, the see-saw variable of tips you
make on any given night, the hard elbows of football dykes—
all keep the colors bright. hey, i could have left town. i could
have moved to Paris. i could have had any number of shit jobs
around the globe and seen the rest of this wild planet and
been the richer for it. but i didn't. i'm here. the archbishop of
rationalization has traveled far in Jamaica Plain. of course one
thing i could NOT do was endure a corporate gig, let alone
qualify for one. up early, home on a cocktail slide, freaking
out the boss with my oddball 'artistic' behaviors. not me. this
is where i am, it's where i belong. the tape has not run out on
what makes the job and the town new, over and over again. i
love it here and i've come to accept that i need to live in one
place long enough to get the art done in a safe harbor. if i
played guitar maybe that would be a different story. you can
carry that thing on your back. but i can't. i look stupid playing anything but a piano. so here i am, a faux-Buddha under a
New England elm tree.

IS THE GRASS REALLY GREENER? (REDUX)

or are we honestly just fine in our own skin? would we, if we could, be anyone other than who we already are? to have the flash money of a Wall Street tycoon, the endless sexual opportunities of a rock star, the way-too-beautiful boy who draws moths to his preposterous flame, the leggy body of the model who walks the runway like 'fuck-you-bitch,' the outsized athleticism of the Olympic swimmer, the impossible leap of a dancer, the oceanic saxophone voice of a black blues singer or the power to move people as poet, novelist, painter, film maker. we lie in bed, heavy with the weight of the not done, the 'all' we may never be, the relationships that are missing or too much with us, the families that drive us crazy, the cars that won't start, the jobs that don't pay enough for the shit we take, the books we never write, the plays we're not in and the races we're too scared to run. we are charged so many debits and collect so few credits. but honest to God, we like who we are, don't we. we like our name, our silly astrological sign, our dysfunctional families, our besotted friends and our peculiar failures. the face that ain't gettin' any younger is still the face that we quietly, reluctantly, love and the way our eyes in the mirror cannot lie. the blur we see in the window as we imagine a younger, hotter self is a soft joke: amusing, familiar and oddly cool. so, when you get right down to it, we wouldn't ever want to be anyone other than who we are, right? the grass 'looks' greener, but it ain't, it's burnt. we own our Dharma path, no one else does. why would we trade that in for the unknown other? we can't and we wouldn't. our soul is not for sale.

SECRETS

'if i tell you this you won't tell anybody else, ok? cuz i've never told this to anybody ever.' i promise when they ask, but why me? is it the Uncle Homo syndrome (he has to be discreet because he had to hide his 'nature' all those early years and will get it about secrecy)? do they unload because i have a rep? i leak and they want it told to others. they want the dead fish pried out of their gut and onto the street. these confessions remind me of the criminal who is driven to tell a girlfriend, a cell mate, a lawyer, a brother so that he or she will unlock him from the prison of his guilt. so yes, sometimes i break my promise. i slip a velvet whisper into a safe ear just because the secret is nasty, funny, or impossible to keep. i insinuate per-mission. on the other hand, i hide a handful of privacies who's lock box has never ever been violated. some are mine, some belong to friends or strangers. they live inside my head like a child hiding in the basement, safe but wary. secrets begin in childhood. they begin the first time you realize that Mom and Dad are not God and that they don't know everything there

is to know about you. they don't see you walk out of a bar-
ber shop with a comic book that doesn't belong to you. they
don't catch you flipping through Dad's Playboy, unmoved by
Marilyn's juicy tits. they don't know what happened between
you and your next door neighbor out in the barn. you are out
of range from Mom and Dad's all-seeing eye of Sauron. this
began for me when i realized that Santa Claus was a fiction,
that he smelled of booze and had a voice like Uncle Karl. i
didn't say anything about it because i hated the truth. i didn't
bring it up with my sisters because they were younger and
living the magic of Christmas. i kept doubt to myself until i
met my first best friend. he was the first person i told things
to i never told to anybody else and with whom i did things i
never did with anybody else. things that were secret. secrecy
is a part of love. my first best-friend was the first person i
ever fell in love with even if i couldn't use those sacred words.
i thought about him when he wasn't around. i felt differently
when i touched his arm and when he leaned against me. i was
hurt when he criticized. my heart leapt when he laughed. it
was the secret of how i was with him that changed me, made
me feel new, re-invented, bursting with light. which is why,
later on, a love affair gets its charge from secrecy, from a
dream world enshrined in a cathedral built, stone by stone,
with the person you love. why, early on, i didn't want to use
the L-word until i was sure. i didn't want to jinx the miracle
with a silly verb. i didn't want my friends to be in on what was
happening or to break love down into shards of demeaning
transparency. if all secrets are known then magic evaporates
in a torch light that exposes worms and rust.

SMALL TALK, BIG TALK

one of my favorite things ever is to have the Big Talk, the
kind of conversation that instead of being an ever-repeating
ego-echo climbs a discovery ladder. each side of the conversation is listened to fully, towering like a Sequoia. when your
side of the conversation is not an internal prep for one's own
commentary or anecdote but where listening is true and
speaking frankly matters. this wild-ride, carnivalesque-jazz
riff over coffee or before the slur hits the booze wall or before
a pot-high paranoia overwhelms the senses is rare indeed and
we know it when it happens. it is here that the appearance of
actual communication infuses the vibe ahead of seduction and
real talk is real. but of late i think, especially at work where
a mere 'hey,' or 'what's new?' or 'good to see you' can carry,
in spite of its cliché, off-the-hook flippancy, it's own sincere,
emotional weight. it is in the eyes. you can read it there and in
voice you can hear it, one's heartfelt interior. i used to disdain
what's-up-dude? shorthand, high-fives, and fist bumps but not
anymore. lately i'm more apt to doubt the depth, the sincerity
of my own late-night spew. i join in with the not-as-simplis-
tic-as-they-seem people who get more out of less, a world out
of a worm. as a friend put it: 'don't say it, be it.'

BROTHERS

i love my sisters. we know each other in that profound way that only time and blood can develop. i depend on them. i never resented their gender or tried to convert them into boys, but i think, as i began, early on, to have boy-crushes, some of those friendships may have been predicated on my desire for a bro. i've always wanted one, or two: someone to compete against, someone older, a sign-post scout, or younger, a kid i could look after and protect. maybe i bought the idea that brothers, when young, fooled around and in sexy inno-cence played with each other or in front of each other and found out what that tent in your pants was all about. but it goes deeper than that. i wanted someone (Dad not being the greatest in the bonding department) to lock-in with, to com-pare notes, to challenge my manhood or dispel/forgive my weakness. if i 'made' brothers (the way they 'make' members in the Mafia) it was with my first friends. we walked the forest, arm-in-arm as if blood-related, brothers by proxy. we could cut a finger, share the cells and belong to a soul river that we self-created. that's how technicolor those first glorified friends translated. i have your back, you have mine. in Lonesome Dove, Augustus McCrae and Woodrow Call are equal to this archetype. neither was complete without the other as a foil, as a measure against himself and as a trustworthy, truth-tell-ing pair of eyes—man-love without sexual rising. that's who i wanted. a Captain Call or a Gus McCrae in the next door saddle. i guess i found them, these part-time brothers past, present and future in the long trail of best friends. they sustain the parts of myself about which i'm ok: loyalty, directness, an open heart, a crazy imagination, a symbiotic view, a foolish leap off the cliff and a willingness to look like shit on any given day.

COLLEGE?

i wonder if we need to go, straight out of high school into the firing line when we're not even sure why, just to move a kid out of the house and onto the dogtrack of binge drinking, shirtless screams at sports cams, getting knocked-up or riddled with STD's, studying at the last gasp on amphetamines with useless info shitting itself out like bad brains into the next-day-exam toilet. the money spent or borrowed is an Empire State Building of debt. we are led to believe that the ladder-climb to success, respect and riches begins with a college degree. but what about the slackers who squeak through high school and are not ready for prime time? why spend the cake? could the Pandora's promise of college life be a let down? could a dull job snap 'real world' hardship into focus and step up a seizure of introspection about what a rightly directed education might prove down the career highway? could this then, and not prematurely, make a cogent blueprint once he or she knows what-the-fuck they really want out of

life? in the days of white shoe, when boys (not girls) joined
the frats their fathers rushed, a hollow leg up the Wall Street
skyscraper could be won with little more than the ability
to get stinko drunk or hit the whorehouse of letter-sweater
intimacy. i for one, as much as college taught me about my
twisted heart, my hidden drives and my obsessive probing
of the withdrawn, burned up Dad's money like a forest fire.
i could have learned as much or more on a tramp steamer or
hitchhiking across Australia. there is something to be said
about testing oneself in the fish stew of peers. to find out with
whom you can catch your breath or learn the odd degrees
of difference or at least scab off the sophomoric whims of 'i
will be a doctor/lawyer/hot shot' as soon as that chemistry
course nails you to the floor. or 'i will be a writer' when at the
bottom of your paper in American Studies in red pencil you
read the comment: 'this is either the best or the worst thing
i've ever read in my life.' but to spend or owe that much money
to learn all the places you fail is false advertising and bought
into, like the credit cards handed out like candy to freshmen,
only to be abused. all these kids gobble up is the pretense of
discipline when on a good day it's really about learning how
to get by, to cheat, to do the least and still make the grade. to
wait until your life finds focus might not be such a bad idea in
hurry-up America.

MY GIRL FRIENDS

have often been my best friends well before 'fag hag' made it
into the cynical repertoire. beginning with high school, the
girl who gave a shit about me, who stood by her closeted pal
was a consistent fact of life. she championed my obsessions, my
trafficking in the emo underworld and my starry eyes about art
and life. we'd become inseparable, interdependant and shared a
worldview with made-up vocabulary, in-joke humor and x-ray
insight. what i overlooked, shamefully, were those rare girlfriends who loved me too much for their own good. who over-
worked our un-sexualized connection even as they knew, heart-
deep, that boy-girl love was not in the cards. they'd listened
patiently to my crush-rants in the same way i'd listened to
straight boys carp about their shitty girlfriends. those unreachable guys i'd mirrored with undivided attention as i (weakly)
camouflaged desire. i became the straight boy in reverse to
my sympatico girlfriend. she'd bit her tongue and consoled
me about the kid who hadn't made it all the way across the
bi-bridge. she had waited and hoped for more of me for herself,
fantasizing that she alone could've delivered the missing link
in my loser love life. we got strung up in some dizzy, parallel
karmic love-trap, a half-requited but not unrequited maze, as
if 'put there' to teach our sophomoric hearts what had not been
learned about full-on soul-connection. we slept in the stale bed
of unequal romance even as we knew, separately, sadly, that we
would suffer. we do that, don't we? choosing in 'best friendship'

someone for whom we feel way more. where the imbalanced heart longs for level ground, longing eyes, erotic touch. it's hard to believe that the person we feel so much for cannot, on their side, feel the same back. i've been super lucky. i've had several astonishing, talented, strong-souled, brilliant women nurture my better self and believe in me with spotlight eyes even as it hurt, even with those whom the barcode scan of drunken locals inspired nasty fiction. 'look at that one. he is SO into his hair,' we laughed. we were side by side. we'd shared art, absurd ambition and disappointment, all until the unguarded heart broke or until i woke up and saw how she'd been let down. or until she threw in the towel and chased after a straight kid who could truly love her back. from these great friendships difficult wisdom grew. i loved them all, i still do, my best girlfriends: those i hurt when i didn't mean to, and those i didn't hurt at all. each of them continue to smile from their perch on an elevated dollhouse stage with a great laugh, head back, getting me getting them. maybe in a distant lifetime we were lovers. maybe we sustain a truer thread by not ever being all that we can be.

COUPLES SYNDROME AND THE WISDOM OF A WISE OLD LADY

what is it about long-time companions who so often, when
out to dinner, don't look at each other, but stare off into the
restaurant, eyes glazed, not speaking. as if all has been
discussed seven times over, or the issue is so difficult to bring
up they say nothing. maybe i'm reading them wrong. maybe
they share a serenity that requires no words but instead,
exquisite silence. then again, wasn't it Nietzsche who wrote
that all relationships, all the good ones, were essentially long
conversations, the cups never dry, the jokes never stale? in
company the stories both have told before still make them
laugh, while sour couples roll their eyes. 'not again,' they
fume. 'i am so tired of his show-off blather.' 'can't she shut
up? she's fucking flirting with that asshole with the same line
she used when she met me.' the isolating desperation of two
as if the other is not in the room, or worse, all too present.
on the flip-side there is the mother of a friend who told my
sister that 'unless you're jealous you're not in love.' and my
friend Jane who used to say, 'they fight like they're in love.'
no tension, no love story. God knows we chew up the initial
emo-rush with dark imaginings. or we stir a tepid pot with
accusation so that the make-up sex is hot, or at least new,
or renewed. it's rare and wonderful to see those few couples,
gay, straight, bi, trans whateverthefuck where life hasn't gone
out of the frame. i remember reading about Bess and Harry

Truman, when they'd moved out of the White House while it was being renovated and were sleeping at the Blair House. the secret service could hear the springs of the bed in the president's suite squeaking like a squawk box. they still loved each other, those two. they still went at it. neither had ever known another. i like hearing that. it keeps me from settling (as if there is a Particular Perfect Someone) just because i don't want to be alone. i see a lot of that 'better someone than no one'-fear of solitude. worse is the nightmare of feeling isolated around the very one you're with. landing in Vineyard Haven, high on acid, my friends Patrick and Sam and i sat at a table at the Black Dog. across from us an old woman was reading. she wore a tight-fitting one-piece gray suit with a zipper that ran from crotch to throat with a ring, like a cock ring, at the neck inviting a pull down. she looked terrific and very old but without the wandering mind, the wistful looks back, the feeling-sorry-for-herself spectre. with my abrupt LSD forwardness i asked: 'how is it, being old?' she put down her fork and looked right at me with clear blue eyes. 'you know what,' she said, 'an old tree, weathered by storm and bleached, is beautiful. we all think so. an old car, up on cinder blocks in a back yard with weeds growing up around a rusted frame is beautiful. we all agree. we love old things. we even collect them. we pay for them. new is nice, but doesn't share the soul quality that has us loving old things, old objects. it isn't like that with people, is it? we like the young. and another thing? you may think, you might hope or imagine that eventually one reaches a plateau where one 'arrives,' finally. where all makes sense

and all questions are answered. well i'll tell you, you don't.
you won't. it's an endless upward curve of learning, suffering,
moving on and trying again. i was married for many many
years. one morning i put down the paper and looked across
the table at my husband who was lost in his breakfast toast,
who was, in a sense, not there. not there with me anyhow. the
sound of his fork on the plate was explosive. that did it. i'd had
it. i left him. i walked out. you see you never know where life
will take you. that no matter how we plan it, no matter what
we anticipate, it will not be that way, not ever. maybe you get
close on a good day, when you're lucky, to having The Truth
fall into your lap. maybe, but not often. ok, that's it. that's all
i've got to say. nice to meet you.' she stood up, pivoted and
left, her cock ring bouncing at her throat.

MIRACLE

i have a friend who believes that everything can be explained
scientifically, that all is chemistry, math, physics. one doesn't
fall in love, one's chemicals interact. one is not inspired, one's
neurons fire ganglions that spark synapses which translate to
'i will paint the library red.' there is no New Age or old age
other dimension, after life or ESP. spirituality is soft brain.
tarot cards are a gypsy mirage. astrology, meditation, prayer,
religion—a fool's fabrication. miracles do not exist. all has an
objective, rational fingerprint understood and languaged by

the mighty mind. i'm in the other camp. an ex-hardcore hippie
who believes that whatever you imagine is 'real.' other dimen-
sionality via drug spoon, déjà vu or dream-triggering song
is sufficient evidence and who can 'explain' love anyway?
Keats, Auden, Bishop—it takes a poet, not an ivory tower.
why clutter up a pretty mind with dirty facts? i defer to a
Van Gogh landscape which was how he 'saw' the fields of
southern France, or the dazzling whirl of stars. i take the
inexplicable as an 'of course.' of course there are both previous
and follow-up lifetimes. of course there is karma in love, in
difficulty, in the dharma bum path of each snowflake-being.
of course there is a soul. of course there are miracles. case in
point: healing a burn on my hand. two weeks ago in a frantic
rush to yank a pizza out of the hopper at work, the hot edge of
the oven door nicked the skin behind my thumb. it curled up
like a window shade snap exposing a pulpy pink spot the size
of a nickel. it made me gag just to look at it. i had a waitress
tape a band-aid over it so it would not get infected or gross
me out. back home i slathered on disinfectant only to learn
that it's best to do nothing, to not cover up, to let the burn air
out, dry and heal. my fabulous t-cells went to work collecting
around the wound like circling wagons, ant-busy and tire-
lessly cleaning, repairing and rebuilding new skin. it took 15
days and itched as i waited. the sting of the work done was a
reminder that something amazing was going on. like
ET healing Elliott with a God-creates-Adam forefin-
ger-to-forefinger touch. the Hollywood miracle became true
blue 'reality' on my hand. i appreciated the happy rehab. i

know, it's all science. any idiot with half a brain could explain
what was up but not me. it was, for this stubborn old bird,
a miracle.

MONEY

freaks me out. supposedly, the 'law of abundance' (Isabel
Hickey-style) claims that if you don't ask for what you don't
need the universe will provide. even as i buy into that, i'm
buying way too much, although my collection of the useless
seems less indulgent than it might be. i buy clothes at Old
Navy. dinner out is Chinese in a bag. my last vacation was
19 years ago and paid for by a dear friend. when i was a kid
i watched Mom pay the bills while the old man in his red
leather chair smoked a pipe and chewed ice on his fifth vodka
tonic. Mum sat at her creaking antique desk, leaning forward,
neck long, writing checks and balancing bills vs income.
i'm like her. i try not to live beyond my means. i refuse to be
held hostage to debt. i don't O.C.D. balance my checkbook,
but i keep a wary eye. i didn't have a credit card for decades
because i'd never bought anything on time. i paid up front or
didn't buy. i loathe the idea of paying money to spend money.
eventually my friend's dad co-signed for a card and now i have
one, which i pay off as fast as i use it. i love the bitch. the sim-
plicity of the hard shiny rectangle. the clarity, tax time, of the
statement. the speed of web transaction. but here's the rub: my

grandfather's father was a millionaire. he lived in a mansion in Rhinebeck, NY. he lost his shirt in the crash of '29 and my granddad, having grown up with dough, with a chauffeur to drive him to school, a) never learned to drive and b) didn't give a fuck about money. his son, my father, felt cheated out of 'the life.' he wanted the show money could buy. Broadway musicals, fancy suits, new cars, a 50's bullshit status with decals of the colleges we went to littering the rear window of his Jaguar. my Mom had a small inheritance that doubled Dad's income so we were ok, just shy of upper middle class. we lived in a big house with nine acres of lawn, had two cars, went to private schools and on big-assed vacations. but we saw how much Dad hated his job at the 'Girard Trust and Corn Exchange' (whose name was shitted out of his mouth like an oily turd). he wished he'd been a writer. he resented Mom's income as a sword held over his neck. my sisters and i never mastered the money game. we scratched out a living, two of us as waiters, one a teacher and none of us making the big grab. this painted us into corners. the fat options money could buy were out of reach but we saw through the charade of vacant materialism, opted for art, life, love and spirit ahead of wallet. we seem happier for it. my sisters have great kids and their lives are full. i don't have a family but i spend my tips making records. i lose money but i love it—it's who i am, it's what i do. i stand tall on the catalogue. i wander afield only on those rare occasions when i want to give a friend a good time and they can't afford it. or if a Democrat has a chance of kicking Republican ass in an election. still, i worry. what will hap-

pen when i'm 'let go' at work? when my measly Social Security
check can't pay the rent, let alone a trip to the movies. i fantasize
about sporting a beehive 'n pencil-behind-the-ear and pushing
a walker around Doyle's 'til the cows come home but without
that, to tell the truth, i'm screwed and toothless in a wheelchair,
drooling onto a linoleum corridor and hopefully so out-of-it on
tranquilizers i won't know the difference. was there ever a time
in history when money had nothing to do with quality of life?
probably not. were this India i would head out onto the dirt path
with a rag around my waist, low balls, a wooden bowl and chase
all the skinny, black-eyed boys who'd have me.

GUNS

scare the shit out of me. i was never the brat with the plastic
holster and a pop gun. i liked Tonto more than the Lone Ranger
and Silver more than either. i played doctor, house and store, not
war. i can count on one hand my encounters with the dark metal:
1) Dad marching into the living room with a Civil War mus-
ket that he strung up on the mantle and that now leans against
my bureau like an exhausted whore; 2) the brass flare gun he
fired into the night sky chasing my sister and her boyfriend
around the block in a jealous rage; 3) the .22 which, along with
my mother's jewelry, was stolen out of our house in Philly. my
parents were away, i was in charge. i brought some inner-city
kids out to the house to drink, smoke weed and go crazy—which
they did (i was probably after one of them)—when Mum and

Dad returned to discover the missing jewelry, the missing .22 and their screwball son. they flipped. weak-kneed courage and guilt carted me down to South Philly to track down the culprits and the loot. i located two of the guys on the street and pleaded with them, 'the shit ain't mine. i have ta get it back. i understand why you took it. i'd been a fool to have you guys out to a house with a lot of stuff around when you have little. i won't call the cops. i just want the shit returned. please.' one of them sent a scout to find their leader. he sent back a message: if i returned the next day he'd hand the stuff over. i did and got it back but the .22 had been sawed off and the punk pointed it at my head, watched me sweat, lowered it and laughed at my silly, tail-between-legs girly idealism. no more social work for Berlin; 4) in Somerville my sister and i met a pyro who'd burned three houses to the ground. we considered adopting him (cross-eyed hearts). i'd met the kid when he was 'working' at the Ritz-Carlton beauty salon at the same time i was wallpapering the back room (this was the same place i unearthed hair rinses with fancy names like 'Frivolous Fawn,' 'White Mink' and 'Chocolate Kiss' that got transformed into the Orchestra Luna's 'Doris Dreams'). he moved in, slept in my bed and enjoyed nights of passive blow jobs and meaningful looks. one day my next door neighbor, the boy i was truly in love with and who'd become jealous of pyro, showed up at the door with a .45 heavy in his hand. i think it was his way of telling me to dump the peroxide blond. i hid it under the mattress until the fire starter left, nervous about the unpredictable scene next door, then within seconds

me and my sister grabbed the gun, walked to the Charles and
threw it in the river—plop; 5) in JP, back from seeing Raging
Bull, stoned, my boyfriend and i walked into the kitchen and
there it was, on the table under the lamp: thick, gray and nasty—a serious piece. it had been put there by some coke dealer
staying the night. i yelled at him to get the gun, and himself,
the-fuck-outta the fucking house or i'd call the fucking cops.
truth be told there were times during the operatic scenes of
my relationship back then when i tried to manipulate my boyfriend under threat of suicide—prima donna Berlin. had there
been a gun lying around i think in a split second of weakness
i might have tried to use it on myself, or worse. so there ya
have it. i hate 'em. i'd love to get rid of 'em. fuck that i-am-a-
real-man-with-a-gun shit. fuck it up the ass.

MY KIA

is a brand-new, moss-green, sparkly 2011 CMV (cunt mama
vehicle?! cytomegalovirus?!) 'Soul/Exclaim!' with all the
implications of those words. i bought it three years ago
and not only did it cost more money than i've ever spent on
anything ever in my whole entire life, it is also the absolute,
very-first car i ever bought, period. prior to that i borrowed
or took a cab or a long-time boyfriend would get something,
a Duster or a shitbox Dart. my Dad bought me a blue panel
truck when i drove to Steamboat Springs, CO to be a half-

assed teacher. my last car was the used GrandAm my Mum
left me after she died. it's still going strong, the motor anyhow, albeit dented up and nutty, but drivable and kicking. i
gave it to my sister. my mechanic promised it'd be good for at
least another 60-90 thou (it wasn't—died soon after arriving
in Albany). still, for 15 years it drove me all over town. the
point is, again, i never bought one myself. i never had to. i
was terrified of the expense, the responsibility, the insurance,
the threat of getting smacked up in traffic. but now, with
Social Security to handle the monthlies, i own this thing, this
car, this object of which i am so fond. oddly it is as if i am in
some over-the-top, obsessive, romantic relationship with a
'thing,' an inanimate. i talk to it as i approach (clicking open
the door from 20 feet away): 'hi.' when i leave, i say 'goodbye.'
when i start to meditate i 'see' it, the face of my beloved, a
misty vision inside my head. it is my friend, my easy lover, my
favorite dog. it even looks like someone i know with its snub
pug-nose. i caress the hood, the dash, the houndstooth uphol-
stery. everything on it works—the windows, the doors, the
gas cap, the sun roof, the electronically-adjusted side mirrors
and the hazards (which i forget to shut off and rush back to
correct). every design choice pleases my snooty aesthetic eye
as if delivered in some rare nirvana cloud by a beloved guru. it
is so quiet with the windows up you can't hear the engine idle
at a stop light. there are so many instrument panel buttons i
lose focus trying to make adjustments on the radio/cd/Sirius
player. the AC kicks in like arctic snow. i can, if i want to, open
the gas cap without leaving the driver's seat (the GrandAm

required a screwdriver). the mileage is green—24 city, 32
highway. the front window is so wrap-around-huge it's as if
i'm in a diving bell with a 360° panorama, an Avatar in a 3-D
future. in the rain the wipers, front and back, work seamlessly
with no scars across the glass. an endlessly-gorgeous, tingling
sensation makes every trip i drive feel like a pot high and
each regular journey a first-time kiss. i don't know when i'm
going to tire of this, if ever. i wish my Mum could have seen
it, she would have loved it, beaming and posture erect in the
passenger seat, proud of me for making such a brave, wise
choice. i can't take full credit. my roommate's girlfriend posed
as my wife. she did her hair up special and wore a fuck-you,
just-try-to-impress-me look to ward off any hardcore sales-
men. in the meantime, she'd already chosen the KIA online,
pricing and comparing it to the other models i checked out,
the Chevy HHR and the Honda Element. we looked at all
three on Motor Mile. the Element was four-square awesome.
its all-plastic interior can be hosed down without spoiling. its
salesperson was a sweet, wet-lipped, mumbler who was the
exact opposite of the sleaze-bag, hotshot Music Man-type
we expected. it was as if he tried to not sell the car. we liked
him. my 'wife' liked him. but the Element, as fab as it was,
was ultimately four G's more expensive than the KIA with
way-worse mileage. the HHR guy couldn't have given a shit.
his shop was greasy and no one there seemed to want to sell
anything to anybody. the car looked cool on the outside, but
was claustrophobic to drive and the steering had a squooshy,
no-control feel. we saw the KIA last at a small Mom 'n Pop

dealership. we test drove a 2010 red, but i was not, under any
circumstances, going to buy a red car and meanwhile the
salesman was a shark but so obviously so that we laughed
him off. the only one available in not-red was a hamster green
2011, loaded (the only 'Soul' on the lot). i had sworn up and
down that the one thing i would not do was buy that same
day. we were just looking, period. i'd brought the 'wife' along
to make sure i kept my promise. but the shark showed his
teeth and offered an awesome deal and wife whispered that it
was too good to pass up and so fuck it, i bought it on the spot
and strangely without a shred of buyer's remorse. i drove it
like a little old lady who's terrified she's gonna hit something
or get hit. eek! i took it all the way out to Watertown to my
favorite car wash so it could be sprayed with protective goo.
i plucked something as small as a single pine needle off the
floor mat and flick it out the window like a booger. i guess it's
the American thing, a dude and his car, except that this one's
Korean, smallish with no leather ball sack under the rear axel
and can be dissed as, in the vernacular, 'gay.' but so-the-fuck
what! i'm in love and when that happens no one can tell you
different. my plan, my hope is to drive it as long as i did the
GrandAm, at which point i'll be 80 years old and they'll want
me the-fuck-off the road. i will fight whomever tries to do
that with brick-in-purse as i hit the gas and crash it through a
store front window.

MY JOB

waiter at Doyle's for more years than i can count. doing
anything this long invites disaster, boredom, wet-brain, mis-
takes, getting shit-canned, psychiatric treatment or criminal
acts. i guess i'm just plain lucky because i love what i do. i did
from the start. i look forward to it every night, even when
my art homework is coitus interrupted and a song is half
boiled on the stove. there are many reasons why i dig the gig.
for one, it ain't phony. yuppies (when they existed) are never
comfortable there. it ain't posh but it has a great vibe and it's
a good time; the food and service are friendly and inexpen-
sive. booths and beer sell the joint to the newly arrived. the
three rooms, from the original antique bar to the 80's addi-
tions, have a family frankness, a we–did–this–ourselves–not–
some–interior–designer–with–ascot–and–little–dog crap. tin
ceilings, wobbly fans, paintings and photos of politicians, Red
Sox teams, high school yearbook portraits taken back in the
mid-20th clutter the space. i like looking around. it appeals
to me in an easy way. the worn-through linoleum, beer neon,
hanging lamps and the recently-added flat screen TVs co-ex-
ist with the sway-backed shelves behind the bar. the kitchen is
huge and crazy-loud with the attack of cooking, dishwashing,
pizza hurling, foul language, frantic expedition and screaming
cell phone calls to kids. the bar is a 25-yard-long slab loaded
with a soldier's salute of beer taps. the murals make no sense.
are we in Boston? Switzerland? Ireland? some are incomplete

(the artist couldn't paint hands and hid them behind Pil-
grim skirts). the Indians are more yellow than red and were
repainted, as was the ceiling, after the smoking ban. during
the cigarette, era the walls and tin accumulated a nicotine
crust. the new paint job holds, translucent as glass. but none
of the above would keep me, or anyone else, working there
all these years if there wasn't more to it. more than whizzing
about the floor, banging through doors, mopping up kids' rice
from the tables or dealing with idiots. it's who you work with
and work for that gets you through the night. i get a bang out
of my co-workers, then and now. they are a rag tag lot and
we, yell, fight, laugh, steal tables, shrug off asshole customers and beat up on them as soon as we're out of earshot. we
squeal/cheer the Sox, Pats, Bruins and Celts. the jokes and
anecdotes never let up or get stale. gossip is as thick as gravy,
complaints wild and the side-work can be spotty. we shrug off
the annoying cliches: 'i'll DO a Hoegaarden' – 'do? are you
serious? should i watch?'; 'i'm still WORKING on my prime
rib' – 'with a screw driver?'; 'can ya get me a glass of water
'when you have a chance'...as in HURRY THE FUCK UP!'; 'i
hated it, hardy har, har, har,' when every plate has been licked
clean. the naughty desert eyes: 'i'll try the mudd pie. tee hee
hee'—like they're remembering some exotic sexual position.
the presumption of the regular who assumes that because he's
been to Doyle's a zillion times, he deserves the extra attention. really? probably. but over time, regulars become friends.
like teachers, we watch their kids grow up. we hear about an
impending divorce, a son's first guitar, a daughter who won a

writing award. the waitstaff is mostly girls. cooks, dishwash-
ers, bartenders—mostly dudes. the kitchen guys hang tough
and are dirty-mouthed and hilarious. when you boom through
the swinging door you enter their turf which is louder, raun-
chier and more real, in a lotta ways, than the 'how can i help
you?' politesse back on the floor. the bartenders open wine
bottles by grabbing the belly in one hand and back-assward
twisting the bottle not the corkscrew. but hey, this ain't the
South End. the girls ain't Vogue sleek or knock-out hot. they
cover a broad age spectrum but are good-looking in that
straight-forward, working-class, what-the-fuck way. we wear
t-shirts, shorts and jeans. there is no snotty have-to-wear-
black dress code. and we're quick. turn over is our bread and
butter. not many customers linger anyway. big families with
lotsa kids running all over the restaurant want in and out in
a snap. the back room is the only function space of its kind or
size in Jamaica Plain. it can handle birthday parties, political
fundraisers, soccer trophy nights, wedding receptions, grad-
uations and hoards of ultimate Frisbee and lesbian football
teams. years ago, Eddie, who bought the joint back in the 60's,
made sure that no prejudice was allowed. he made it a rule:
if some asshole was racist or homophobic, he was banned for
life. who knew that a liberal agenda was gonna take over the
hood? dykes love Doyle's. so do cops, veterinarians, African
Americans, indie rockers, Germans, nuns, Haitians, students,
socialists and trans-people. the polyglot is happy here. there's
no paid vacation, sick or maternity leave. you show up or you
don't and you make the money you make, but you walk outta

there with your tips, you can adjust your schedule to suit
another occupation and you don't take the job home. i rarely
hang after work. i love the interplay and frenzy during my
shift, but i don't feel like sticking around later (i have other
friends at another bar). but ya know what? when things get
tough, we count on each other. we pitch in. we pass the hat for
someone who's sick or who's lost a friend, having a birthday or
getting married. we read with a glance how waitress X is handling the asshole at table 30 and we have her back. regulars
have nicknames: 'the dog lady,' 'the basketball guys,' 'why do
you DO that?' we laugh about them. we have to. it's like that
in 'the industry' and especially at Doyle's. it ain't corporate
and that's why it's fun, that's why it works and that's why so
many of us have stayed on. my sister, a waitress for years, said
'you can't be yourself when you wait tables.' i get it and acting
does happen at Doyle's, but it ain't Shakespeare and you can
pretty much be who you are. you can even have a count-your-
farts-in-the-hallway contest with Kelly and Sheila, or do the
crossword when it's dead slow. that's just part of why the place
is awesome, why there are so many returnees ('are you still
here?'), why so many of the staff have stuck around and why
i'm grateful to have the gig. hey, they even call me 'Ricky.'

THE OLD LADY

in the back room has one good eye and one fucked-up eye.
she's all chicken bones in a house dress, frail and helpless. she
needs to be led around by the elbow. she doesn't want a cocktail, she wants coffee. she helps herself. the bad eye is watery,
poked-out and unseeing, a scary, egg-white blob. i wonder if,
in an earlier century, she would have been accused of practicing the black arts, run outta town or burned at the stake.
she doesn't say much. she's in her own world. at times it's as
if she's not there at all. friends and family speak to her or at
her. how is she doing? she looks at her loafers. she waits until
they finish with their attentions. i imagine her young, pretty,
flirting but it's a stretch. i see her in her kitchen under a harsh
fluorescent light, the dishes piled-up and befouled, a smell of
piss and toast crumbs on the formica. definitely a bad-picture
TV with the sound on low, her slippers worn at the heel and
the photos of relatives turned over. a sickly cat is curled up in
a corner. i hope i got her wrong. i hope she's aware, safe, living
in her own house, taking calls and sky-high on pills.

PATIENCE

does not become me. i try to slow down, to wait ('they also
serve…'), but i'm terrible at it. i rush through songs, i tick
off my list for the day like a housewife on meth. i meet new

people and crash course their autobiography. at work i smack
the plates down on the table even as i try, so help me, to gently settle the food onto the paper mat. driving cross country
i count not miles, but states, hurtling through the imaginary
dotted lines that atlas-separate Kansas from Iowa. i drink beer
like water at a just-made-it oasis. i eat shovelfuls of Chinese
and suck up Pu Pu like a Hoover. perhaps i am racing towards
the end of my life. or maybe i'm trying to see, touch, experience, absorb everything and everyone in my path as quickly
as possible so as to not miss anything. i watch myself roar
down the road in fifth gear but it never slows me down. i rev
the engine, i lurch through life. Buddha would have a problem
with me.

BLOODY SHAVE

at one point i had free access to a gym. a 30th-floor, downtown health spa filled with chrome machines, mirrors, men
and women sweating off pounds and working hard to transform flubbery bodies into generic, cut, hairless 'beauty.'
nothing more absurd looking than a rock hard 20-year-old
body sprouting a 45-year-old head. i pretty much got nowhere
fast. there were no pounds lost, no change in body contour. i
went because it was, for a few short months, free and it got me
out of the non-profit office where i holed up. what stayed with
me was an unforgettable sight. in the shower everyone keeps

an eagle-eye perimeter around their naked selves. 'i'm naked. you're naked. i see you, but i'm not looking at your dick and for fuck's sake, don't look at mine.' one afternoon i'm toweling off at the sink while the guy next to me is shaving. he has a big, slap-happy grin but his face is covered in blood. the blade has sliced up his neck, throat, cheeks and Adam's apple. i can't believe what i'm seeing until i get it—he's blind. the guy is fucking blind! here he is, 30 years old, 30 stories up, towel around waist, shaving in a public bathroom. shaving blind and bloodied-up ecstatic. the freedom he feels, unassisted, shaving himself thoroughly rips me out of my bleak cynical judgement. what a dude. what an amazing, amazing guy. i didn't say a word. i just admired how incredibly awesome he was.

STARING AT STUFF

i see them, wandering away from a party in the restaurant, up and down on toes and heels in the hallway, staring blankly at posters, memorabilia and artifacts. it is as if they don't feel like small-talking or managing a birthday moment or being pushed about by a friend or family member to participate. they want outta there, but can't leave, so they wander and gaze like giraffes at anything not human. that's one version. the other is the small-town tourist i imagine driving a gigantic stainless steel RV, traveling the USA and stopping to gape at every scenic view. they have to take a picture to memorialize what is to me impossibly boring. and so, at Doyle's i see them, wrists clasped 'round the back, squinting at all that crap on the walls as if it tells them something vital, something which, if they missed it, would become an existential loss.

THE GRIM SMILE

looks like this: lips tighten, the corners of the mouth curve down and the chin puckers—all in one simultaneous gesture. we all do it. i do it. famous people do it. politicians on TV do it. i never fully took this in until i saw Bubba, in his empathetic prime, put that face on, the grim smile. he had me believe him even when i shouldn't have. the grim smile says a million things: 'i hear ya'; 'i'm humble'; 'my heart goes out to you'; 'i acknowledge my mistake'; 'you caught me in a lie'; 'don't worry, you'll be fine.' if you add a nod, it communicates a deeply felt 'yes.' if you move your head from side to side, it becomes: 'what can i say? ya got me.' it's a con. it's also the truth. where did these muscles learn to do this? i see kids doing it, imitating parents. is it ingrained, a signal developed as early as cave men guilt? was there a cave man Bubba? i can't stop myself from doing it even if i wanted to. still, i wish it weren't so automatic. God, i'm doing it now even as i type.

SMALL DETAILS

of the day—the laundry, taking out garbage, making the
bed, clumping cat shit out of the litter box, getting the list of
to-do's crossed off one by one at day's end. groceries, vitamins, idiot shopping, dishes, vacuum, phone calls, emails,
twarts, bills paid—they are endless and they keep me in
line. my lumbering 69-year-old body likes doing housework
minutiae, holding insanity at bay with regularized chaos.
'i do, therefore i am.' 'clean up your room and make your
bed. it will quiet the blues,' my best friend's mom, Weastie,
admonished (she later sat in a car, garden hose from exhaust
to window and killed herself). so i wonder how i will handle
NOT being able to look after everything. not being able to
wipe my own ass. will i lose it? will i be able to bear, let alone
ask friends and family to handle the detritus of my day? will i
stand for it? will i not want others to be at my beck and call?
why clutter up their lives with my clutter? or will i become a
stinko curmudgeon like my Uncle Andy and chase help out of
the apartment with a cane?

BUT I THINK, THERE'S SOMETHING TO BE SAID FOR, YOU KNOW, LIKE, I MEAN... ER...

was the brain stall i overheard the other night at work. he was fishing around, like a hand in a jammed-to-the-gills purse, for the thought he wanted to get out of his head. as if by using catch phrases as lures he could somehow hook the evasive idea and yank it to the surface. his friend hardly seemed impatient. maybe he too had a line in the water near an algae-softened sneaker. it was hilarious to hear, to even notice. i stumbled away with a pitcher of water trying not to burst. we are so funny when we try to stab the dark with a dull dart.

SHE

came through the front door of Sorella's and was moving with short, quick steps towards Ellie, the owner, whose new hair after chemotherapy had grown back with thick, dark-brown poodle curls. Ellie reminds me of the Basque woman in For Whom the Bell Tolls. she is a Hemingway two-by-four of a woman who is so sure of herself she's sexier than any hot chick in the room. she stares fear in the face and scares it off

the stage. her features are large—big lips, big smile, big legs,
big bulk. on holidays she dresses up. she's a Gypsy. she's Ma
Joad. i don't know much about her except on Sundays when
most of the time she lets me take the small, one-person
window seat where i can read and shovel in a Romeo omelette.
the woman speaking with her today looked like a lesser
version of Ellie. she was more tightly wound. the radar eyes
i was sure she had even though i couldn't see them bore into
my skull, straight through Ellie's body. she wore short shorts
that hugged a middle-aged ass, too-tan legs, sandals and a
brazen show-her-tits blouse. i wonder about women her age.
do they stop worrying about no longer being young? do they
worry about it as much as older men do? or differently? then
i forgot about her. i went back to Gone with the Wind and
Scarlett O'hara who at 17 had been through more life than
most ancients, a wicked girl with wicked thoughts who made
you want to know her for real, to crank up the movie version and see those startling green eyes. then i became aware
that someone had stopped at my table. it was her, that weird
woman, staring at me with a curious smile. her blood-red-
lipstick lips parted as if in her mind she could read mine. how
did i look to her, eyes over glasses, fat book in my lap with the
disturbed desert dry hair? had i been Fellini i would have cast
her instantly as a drive-by wench, or madam. someone i could
count on to yell at the top of her lungs in a desperate scene
in a movie i would never make. she was there barely seven
seconds and then floated away in an eddy of hot afternoon
air. she confirmed my New Age theory that we, as souls, are

destined to meet all souls belonging to us, if only for a split second, for a glimpse or long term but meet them we must before we die. they teach us, as we teach them back, the ineffable big book truths about everything we know nothing about.

BUSTED IN GRENADA (ABOVE AND BELOW: THE JANEEN)

1970. learning to act at the Yale Drama School (same time Meryll was there). starting to hate it. the perpetual 'one's body and one's self is one's 'instrument' and one needs to practice 'it' all the time' was turning me inside out: 'practicing' accents, facial tics, postures. my friends wondered what-the-fuck was going on with Kinscherf? why does he seem so fake? when i heard that a friend of a friend of mine, a pot dealer from Amherst College, was shooting a movie in the West Indies and that i could have a part, it was the nudge i needed. i dropped out of Yale and got my pal Francesca to hop on the bus, bounce outta New Haven and fly on Amherst's dime to the Caribbean. tough call, right? we taxied cross-island to one of several pink bungalow beach houses, were given our own rooms, our own Vespa scooters, our own cars to share and all the food, booze and drugs we could foie-gras-choke down. our homework the first week: 'familiarize' ourselves with the island. this meant getting stoned, drunk, tripped-out and pirate tanned on our own private postcard-perfect beach. two

crescent halves forming a white sand/black sand middle
finger insinuating out into the Gulf with a chubby lighthouse at
the fingernail tip. its beacon—a favorite LSD drop spot where
kaleidoscopic film clips spit-fired out of gonzo foreheads. deep
in the jungle we skinny-dipped in waterfalls, parrots swoop-
ing overhead, banana clusters plopping like puppies into our
sated laps. seafood spreads and rum cocktails paraded on the
cheap in open air St. Georges casbahs. natives laughing (at us?
with us?). this was paradise and it was all ours all the time.
one week in and against the inky blue-black of a starry starry
night a sailboat, our sailboat, the schooner Janeen (re-named
and re-painted The Sad-Eyed Lady) edged past the psychedelic lighthouse and dropped anchor in our tiny personal bay.
a two-masted monster, tip top lights winking, full crew in
dress whites, galley with a chef from Paris, lobster, steak and
champagne on ice—the works. we were oared out to eat, drink,
smoke, dance, whatever, not caring what-the-fuck this movie
was about or when we would begin to shoot it. we were surfing
an infinite rainbow. being here now was an induced reality.
one night our main man from Amherst gathered us round and
told a story, obliquely and slo-mo stoned. the plot: we were
21st-century pirates chasing leftover refugees after an earth kill
nuclear freeze. our orders: seize any ship or person caught in
the crosshairs. that was it?! who cared? we were down for the
count. i became 'lookout,' awarded an all brass telescope which
i polished obsessively and had macraméd by a Grenadian hippie
so that i could wear it like cutlass. arrgh! i loved the thing.
wore it all over the place, 'getting into character' drug-induced

Actor's Studio-style. the first shot on the first day was of me, naked, at the top of the mid-mast spyglass-spotting a mom-'n-dad sloop with a teenage daughter who was booty bounty. that girl, Janie, was (not certain about this) the girlfriend of our benefactor and possibly the muse for his film-to-be. but who knew about anything for sure? i can't emphasize enough that we were, most of us most of the time, skyscraper high on vitamin LSD. that first day of the shoot i saw below my dangling legs, a deck so miniaturized it looked like a toy boat bobbing in a bathtub. when we cut through a 50-yard-diameter-dart-board oil slick so astonishingly beautiful my eyeballs hurt, i wanted to dive into the shimmering bull's eye and shapeshift onto a mountaintop in Nepal. seriously. at night we skinny-dipped in a phosphorescent sea so manifest that swimming felt like flying. or like finger painting. we'd anchor in St. George's harbor, motor a dingy into town and get more fucked up and more outrageous by the minute. we set up a full band on deck and blasted endless iterations of 'Satisfaction' 'cross town, our girls topless. usually topless. all this behavior occurring without complaint. case in point: a young chiquita, a Grenadian, had herself rowed out to The Sad-Eyed Lady to see what was happening. just a kid, no more than 16 wearing a sequined Carmen Miranda pineapple turban with three rattlesnake maracas in each tight fist, eyes flashing. her name, i kid you not, Helen Of Troy Eleanor Roosevelt Nielson. her mom, a Grenadian, her dad a shipping baron from across the pond in Holland. Helen glommed onto us like a starfish, flitting in and out of our orbit and adjusting to our weirdness as best she could. as did handsome Australian sailor boys who, like us, wanted to gulp down the full feast of booze, weed, acid and hash that was all over the compound. 20th-century world-weary refugees who pulled into Port Wherever, worked, partied, fucked and then, after they had enough, hired onto a new rig, a new ocean, a new port. 'round and 'round the globe—a moveable feast, Aussie style. as much as any time in our lives this was heaven on earth, wild, heart-throbbing freedom all too soon to end. around the third/fourth day of the filming as i was monkey-ing about in the rigging, the one boat Grenadian 'Navy' putt-putted into our slip stream, armed and megaphoned. the charges: drugs and nudity. both true. we were whisked off the Janeen, driven to a dank, up-island prison (nerves on edge now that the drugs and booze had worn off) and dumped into a two-room, cinder-block jailhouse. boys in one hole, girls in the other. tin buckets to piss and shit in. the trial set for the next day. one minute, drug blind in our prefab nirvana, the next, incarcerated. and the next? court. would we be trapped and raped here for life? not to be. lucky result: Helen of Troy Eleanor Roosevelt Neilson's cousin, a guy named Maurice, signed on as our defense. he painted us as unwitting victims from good, American homes having innocent fun who had been caught at an awkward, unguarded moment. we were on a plane early the next morning. Helen came along for ride. she got married in Boston a few weeks later and became Helen of Troy Eleanor Roosevelt Nielson Parker—my dad Dick, her best man. the rest of us fled to a house by a river in Greenfield, MA, paid for and outfitted, again, by our pirate king. the plan:

start a band and get famous fast. more acid, more weed, more
insanity until one night, driving back from Janie's house, i
saw flames roman-candling the night sky. Plan 2, a one and
done. coda: our lawyer, Maurice, was elected Prime Minister
of Grenada. in 1983, the island was invaded by Castro Cubans
and Maurice was assassinated. Reagan sent in the Marines
making tiny war history. i moved to Somerville, started my
first band Orchestra Luna, and wound up living in the same
damn town for the next 40-plus. no more Kerouac road trips.
coup de gras? Helen is now Helen Of Troy Eleanor Roosevelt
Nielson Parker Spielman and lives in Hawaii. the movie? atro-
phying in a freezer somewhere in Brooklyn.

MISS PAMELA RUNNING IT ON LIKE IT IS

Pamela said that about three years ago she was with this guy
and all of a sudden she became known as Pamela-and-this-
guy and she wasn't Pamela anymore. she wants to wake up
in the morning and be loving somebody, but she wants to be
Pamela. 'i don't know, Richid. it's hard to explain, but now
that he's a quadriplegic he's brought us all together. we were
all real confused about who we were, our identities. you know
J was our leader in a way and now he's all caught up in being
gay. gay in Santa Fe and he's living with Tommy who's only
eighteen but they've been together for years now because J

does everything for him. he doesn't have to lift a finger. but it's strange, Richid, now that Steve broke his neck and is a quadra...have you ever seen what they do to people who break their necks, Richid? i've never been around someone who's that sick. it makes you go through your whole life. you wonder what matters anymore. you know what i mean? they screw this metal strip that looks like a halo on his head and they have him with weights pulling on his body. one's twenty-four pounds and the other is thirty-six. and then they have him on a waterbed, like and they have to turn him over every two hours. on his back and then on his face, Richid. i've never seen anything like it. he hasn't really slept for a month because they keep turning him over. he doesn't even seem to realize what happened to him. he's been on morphine. he's so sick but he's pulled us all together. everyone from Reddington. does that sound right? people we haven't seen for months are sending flowers from Pennsylvania and New Jersey. and he asks for Michael Weaver. they were good friends. didn't separate over nothing heavy. just straight with each other. Steve told Michael everything real blunt. his doctors are real happy because we all go to see him a lot and we know what to do about not eating milk or too much carbohydrates. so i'm getting involved with cripples. can you believe it? i stare at wheelchairs and i can tell right away if it's a good one or not. and i'm working in volunteer therapy. i'm going to get my hair cut, Richid. i figure now's the time because of the storm. i got to change my hair. i'm gonna get it cut like Peter Frampton. i was down in Beacon Hill during the storm. i was dressed in rags. i looked like shit. everybody

else down there dressed to kill in their pleated pants and i
was a mess. i feel like the Queen of the Subways now, Richid.
i should enter Miss Subways in New York because all i do is
ride them back and forth. i got to move to the North End so
i can walk around a little. i'm cleaning houses in Revere, a
couple of them, and i'm always on the subway and i was in a
movie, Richid, a TV-movie that was on last week with Joanne
Woodward. i was hanging out with her and she's real nice and
Paul Newman's short but he's got those beautiful eyes and all
we did was walk and walk up and down the street and then
run. in all movies they hire people for ten dollars-an-hour
just to walk. i'm going to be in another one. i forget the name
of it. i woulda got involved with Danny who's been teaching
me a lot about how to massage people with injuries and we're
real close, but i won't do it because what's the point of getting
involved with someone when you might run off to California
or something? it don't make sense. i'll call you, Richid. give
me your number. people still remember that song, my song,
but call me Richid because you know i lose things and forget.
the snow has been something here in Charlestown. we had
no oil or heat for days but then the oil man came and gave
everyone a little oil. he was real nice, Richid. Joey is fourteen
now and sometimes, you know, once a week i feel like i never
want to talk to him again because he gets real nasty. he's
real skinny and he isn't interested in girls yet and he's lifting
weights and he got a scholarship to all the Catholic High
Schools that was ten kids out of seven hundred and he didn't

tell anybody. that's the way he is, Richid, he never tells us anything, but he's doing real good and i think he can't decide whether to go into professional sports or to become a heart surgeon. yeah. i should go now too, Richid. yeah. i love you, Richid. Bye.'

OBLIVIOUS

Tom (RIP) reminded me about that time i laid one down at the Choate School, when the Howard Ave New Haven Collective went there for Franny's gig. God knows why they asked her to play. it seemed incongruous. she was a way more intense song writer than the place could have anticipated. regardless, they offered up a buffet dinner at the headmaster's house. soggy paper plates of oozing shepherd's pie atop knees tight together, tinkling china, stale coffee, plastic cups of Cott's ginger ale. i was in another room banging away on a low-boy upright. it was my John Lennon scream-therapy Gestalt period. lots of cruel hard truth and absurdist lyrics, lost in my delirious soundscape, mesmerized by the paradise of boys. late for din-din. Tom said everyone was sitting around on their thumbs when i came back in, did a quick spin, a twist at the waist, raised one leg high, like a figure skater and fired one off. ten seconds of reverent silence followed. oblivious, i moved in on the pie of the shepherd and loaded up.

A PINK INFERNO

we file off the Summerthing truck and go out behind the
Hatch. Orchestra Luna outdoor gig on the Esplanade. someone is blocking the way. it takes a second to figure out who
it is. uh oh. it's him. Dante, our former voice coach ('an 'e' is
like a carrot!' 'Lisa, try this: belt out Everything's Coming Up
Roses on an elevator full of people. it will get you past stage
fright.' she did. i was there). we take turns embracing. he has
tears in his eyes. he's wearing glasses but the tears stain his
cheeks. his beer belly is taut under a pullover, blue-velour
sport shirt. it pushes against me. a quick european peck on
both cheeks, chubby hands grip my shoulders. he's wearing
sandals, thin, white ankle socks and bermuda shorts. they
have a tiny, light blue duck print. 'are these your underwear,
Dante?' (my weak joke.) 'not yet, baby, but they will be soon.'
(i never get his humor.) it is remarkable that he came to see us.
he never goes out for this sort of thing. he has to be escorted
everywhere. hand held. 'i cancelled four students. new ones.
they'd been waiting months. but I said 't'hell with 'em.' i had
to come. i had to be here. to hear you and it was lovely. a wonderful show.' and then an aside: 'i noticed that six, five, one
progression running through your music. da da daaa...lovely.
a lovely motif. it's there, isn't it?' 'oh yes,' i lied, not knowing
what the fuck he was talking about. he stepped back to look at
me. a long affectionate sincerity straight into my eyes. 'listen,
baby. i'm sorry about what happened. it just wasn't working

out. the lessons. am i right? there was no point in going on.'
(we would wait in the ante chamber at his south end studio for
hours to see him. the 'lesson' would would last an hour, most
of which was consumed with his personal memoir. 'Fellini's
ROMA?' jerking off in the car with your friends at night?
'the story of my life, baby…' etc.) 'i think of you. i think of you
often.' 'we think of you too, Dante.' 'do you?' 'yes.' 'goodbye
baby. people are waiting for me.'

¶

MAGOO

"Je est un autre."
— *Arthur Rimbaud*

MATCH ANTHROPOMORPHIZED

i took an angry had-to-get-the-fuck-out-of-bed-early-AM
dump, one of those stinko dark black evacuations. a skunk
turd emanating repulsive sulfurous fumes. i struck a cheerful
match to suck up the stench, flush and uh oh, not good, not
good enough. another match, a flame burst and ate up the
slimy oily air and as i dropped the dead match into the toilet,
i noticed that it was too heavy to float. it sank to the edge of
the hole, to the precipice. it looked lonely as if it knew it was
on its miserable way out. like Orpheus i looked down when i
shouldn't have and i saw it, the match as Euridice, she can't
return because now i've seen her and she'll turn to stone with
no trip back to Paradise. my match ='d Euridice and looked
sad, like the friend i was talking to the other night who saw
no way out of his dilemma.

SPIT SHINE

my approach to cleaning house has never been thorough.
ask Charlie. 'you never really wash the dishes,' he would say,
pointing out spots on the glasses or a stray shoelace of pasta
under a plate which he would then rewash with his nose in air.
at the same time i have a snob's abhorrence for slobs, appearance ahead of truth (at least have your fucking house LOOK
clean, i snark). for me it has always been about aesthetics. i

like the look of a clean, apparently orderly apartment.
it pleases me, like table lamps coloring rooms with a cozy/
sleazy, fantasy-world Blanche Dubois ambience. as for the
dishes, i burn them clean, a lazy, green-less sterilization that
leaves the tap on it's hottest dial, the steam blurring the
window above the sink, until the dish is cooked. oddest idio-
syncrasy: the spit shot. i lob a gob onto an annoying smudge
on the kitchen linoleum and rub it away with toe of my foot-
in-sock while i'm on the phone multitasking like a meth mom.

CAT ABRASION

my dermatologist, Dr. W, a no-nonsense clinician, checks
everything out. Everything. and on each visit. 'take off all
your clothes and put this on, with the opening at the back.' my
frog legs stare up at me. i wonder if i wiped properly earlier
that morning. would i 'leave something' on the paper covering,
a human stain? she is nonplussed and orders me about like a
sergeant, squirts suspicious, asymmetrical spots with an ice
gun. it hurts, but in an ok way, like picking a scab or getting a
tattoo. i'm here for good reason—my skin. when i was in Nas-
sau my sophomore year at Yale, on a drunken-singing-group
spree, i got grotesquely sun burned water skiing off Lyford
Cay (they were shooting Goldfinger that year). i was dart-
ing about on a single ski—whoosh whoosh—when a shark's
fin broke the surface a few yards behind me—a great white

as i recall through the filter of Jaws and selective memory. i
angled towards the pearly beach, flapping one hysterical arm
and coasted up onto the sand as the monster slithered back
out into the briny deep. that was the half of it. it turns out
that the sun, reflecting off the Caribbean blue, carved up my
skin like a laser. i grew blisters the size of robin's eggs. i bled.
we didn't know it then, the latent horrors of Melanoma. my
Mum needed postage stamp sized patches of skin removed
periodically. i notice divots on the noses of customers my age
at Doyle's. on my last visit, instead of the freeze-offs, Dr. W
prescribed a tube of 'Carac' (where do they get these names?)
which i was instructed to apply daily for a month. slather it
on, rub it in, wait. miniscule homing cells in the sauce would
zero in on potential pre-melanomas, stimulate anti-bodies
and eat up the nasty spot. you itch and you develop lesions
that look like leprosy. you are not allowed dressings to cover
them up. you look scary. the hard part is that with this stuff
on my arms, back of hands and the upper side of my face, my
cat can't lick me. 'NO, SOFI, NO!' i ward her off. the poor
girl's confused and hurt. who knew that a slow shark in the
water would have a debilitating psychological effect on my cat
50 years later, to say nothing about the idle kid at the end of
the bar with whom i strike up the band. the one who averts
his eyes because the pus-oozing sore on the back of my hand
makes him want to puke.

WEARING THE HABIT

i repeat myself over and over and over again. i pretend that i
don't. that i am a creative person 24/7. i try to break habits, to
prove that i reinvent everything all the time, but the truth is
i can't help it. try as i might to change, i get bent out of shape
in a heartbeat and revert to repetition. this is most apparent
in the shower. the recipe: 1) turn on spigot, wait for heat to
rise and piss in the tub while standing outside; 2) reach and
blend cold with hot to a scalding, burn-yourself-clean blast; 3)
step in, first left foot then right, face hard rain, squeeze eyes
closed against spray as it hits hair line, cupped hands in front
of face to repel Niagara, hair in face then shoved up and back,
a quick flip landing collected water in the like a bitch slap; 4)
shampoo leaving suds on top like a frilly cap; 5) lather face,
in prep for easy shave; 6) soap up, upper shoulders, pits, arms,
tits, nipples, legs, balls, cock, under ass, ass crack and asshole
having turned with back facing nozzle; 7) scrape off excess
soap, bend over, pull cheeks apart, douche asshole, check for
shit specks in the teeth of the bath mat, tweeze out and nudge
them down reluctant drain; 8) rinse shampoo and squeeze off
excess water; 9) lazy susan back into steam, admiring impressionistic bathroom wall art; 10) twist chrome knobs hard shut,
drag shower curtain to the right and towel off in a predictable
order: face, hair, pulled ears, head and neck, pits, upper arms,
torso, back, ass, legs and feet. i've tried reversing the procedure: feet, legs, asshole, ass, arms, etc—but it fucked me up.

i'm trapped in the cage i built. i wonder what other parts
of my life's assembly line repetition owns. i wonder if any
live-in relationship could survive these set-in-my-ways
parameters. it's way too late. i fancy myself an improviser and
i am a latin teacher: 'repetitio est mater studiorum' (repetition
is the mother of students).

NOSTRIL YOGA

when i catch cold and sometimes when i don't, i have a
serious which-nostril-to-breathe-out-of freak out. one works,
the other doesn't. the working one clogs, the other one's clear.
a needle thin stream of air bites and burns the roof of the
back of my mouth. i try everything. i lie on my side with one
sheet-fold covering the open nostril. i lie on my back with my
head under covers (forcing my cat the-fuck-out of the way).
i press the clear nostril hard into the pillow at just the right
angle to allow for some-but-not-too-much air. i twist a wad
of tissue into a cork and plug. i open my mouth making my
lungs happy even as this provokes cotton mouth. if all else
fails i sit up and read until i'm exhausted enough to not give
a shit about what a disaster the entire situation has become. if
i were a shaman or a guru or a disciple i'd know for sure that
this was an opportunity to practice yoga breath, elevate my
consciousness and 'arrive.' don't breathe, be happy.

RAGE DICHOTOMY

when i was a teenager one of the seniors at my high school,
a kid named Castigliano, punched me in the face twice and
shoved me into a swimming pool for 'foul-mouthing his girl'
(why do we never forget these things?). i had no idea what
he was talking about. i'd had maybe five beers and was just
standing there, at the edge of the oval pool, zit-faced, nonplussed and oblivious. that's when Castigliano clocked me.
springing into action, before the second hit, i clenched my
fist. i was gonna give him the goods for sure, but i...ah...didn't
have the balls. my arm froze. ok, he was bigger, stronger
and nastier than i was, but the picture in my head of my fist
slamming into his pretty jaw disarmed me. i couldn't hurt
him, or was afraid to, or so i told myself, or, or, or. my friends
yanked me out of the chlorine, dabbed at the cut on my face
and consoled me but i never got over it. i whimped out, a total
wuss. this confuses me today because i'm such a sicko, badass,
steroidal motherfucker on the turnpike. any asshole hugging
the bumper of my old lady Grand Am and i hang in there like
a mule, 20 mph over the limit, a wall of traffic in the right
lane, a stream of cars behind me and this bastard can go
fuck himself. i revel in the phantom violence. i will not give
one bloody inch. when at long last there's an opening on the
right for me to scoot into and let the cunt pass, i ignore it. i
even slow down a bit just to piss him off, hit the gas and then,
lurching ahead, smile my most vindictive smile. this fucking

fuck will not pass my fucking gay-assed red car! i play chicken with 16-wheelers, six pack pick-up trucks and Mercedes elitists. this is a silly, lethal contest of wills that i choose to game, cool in my cocoon, white knuckles on the wheel, on fire with clenched-jaw. i become the total opposite of the girly boy at the pool who was too chickenshit to fight back.

BAD BURGERS

i am lying prone in the dentist chair for a new crown to replace one 30-years-decrepit with decay. the doc says i have 'long roots' which is why i need not one but three hits of Novocaine or else i'll flop around in the chair like a beached trout. the temporary insert is plastic. 'chew on one side until you get the new one,' he advises. back home, the drug worn-off, my jaw throbs. the left side of my mouth can't smile, drool drools out and it hurts to open. eat something, you'll feel better i tell myself like a Jewish mother. i check the Food Wall menu to find something tofu soft and then rethink. ah ha! there's leftovers in the fridge from the barbecue last Sunday. i toss out the chicken (which smells like dead mouse) and accept the frozen tomatoes, brown lettuce and two ok burger pat-ties. i tease out a crusty bottom-of-foot-yellow bun. i plop the patties into the Teflon skillet i bought my roommate months ago, replacing his old one. the surface was so scarred it looks totally un-Teflon, violent scrapings impossible to scour clean.

i tap in some garlic powder and pepper and cover the pan with
a glass lid. it seems as if it's gonna take awhile to get cooked
so i drift back to the piano to work on something, losing
track until i smell something nasty. it's the burgers. fuck! at
first i hop (finger to chin): 'hmm... they must be ready.' but
the kitchen's a disaster, the pan is in flames, smoke is billowing like a dust storm and the burgers have transmogrified
into rock-hard charcoal briquettes. i click off the burner and
yank the pan clear just as the smoke alarm squawks, a robotic
female voice: 'fire! fire!' smoke fills the kitchen and hallway. i
flip on the porch fan to suck it out. it crashes to the floor. my
cat skitters down the hall, her hind legs like dragon fly wings.
i reset the fan, the smoke dissipates, the alarm gives up and
i construct a sorry assemblage of bun, 'blackened' burger, a
sliver of bad-smelling cheese, two tomatoes, a slab of lettuce
and a squish of ketchup. i had to chisel the burgers off the
pan. a hammer would have helped. i eat the bed i made. i eat
the embedded teflon too. i shuffle down the hall and fire up
the latest episode of The Wire. i inhale my chemical dinner,
careful to keep everything to one judicious side of mouth. later
on, washing up, i realize i'd destroyed the new Teflon and will
have to buy another, but hey, not all homos can cook.

TAR, BABY

it seems all over town that Mayor-for-life Menino is repaving
the roads. smooth, unlined sleek black rivers that car tires
become quiet on. paving trucks flood stretches of the formerly
bumpy with a bow-shaped tide of warm sticky sweet-smelling
oily tar. at night, with few cars on the road, it's like lake water.
you skim the surface, cutting no wake. the purr of engine,
the muted drone of tires takes you back 50 years when cars
and roads owned Eisenhower America and the wild whoop-
ing freedom of the forever-teenager hopped into souped-up
jalopies and gunned it from town to town. i swell up a bit
after work, one cheap beer buzzing in my ears, when the old
pavement succumbs to the new, the bad skin blasted away
like a dermabrasion treatment. 'work done' on the city gives
us a temporary stay on whatever debilitated horrors the sick
economy has in store. the last glass of champagne before the
besotted lunatic jumps out of a twenty-story window.

POKE THROUGH

thin toilet paper (carefully accordioned) can split open on
your way 'in' and a chocolate brown half moon collects under
a horrified fingernail. smell-check confirms the worst. you
swear this will never happen again (it does). on your next trip
to the supermarket you examine labels for guarantees: super

strength, multiple layering, 'no poke-through' as subtext.
you wonder if this is a common accident or are you the
singular exception? come on, tell the truth. have you ever
poked through? you can say.

SARDINES

i don't get to fly much, at least not in the last 20 years. i liked
airplanes as a kid. my little boy brain obsessed over the undulating porpoise backs of those four-prop TWAs. the Ipana
stewardesses patting my head, fluffing pillows, pouring coke
over ice cubes gave me the shivers. the scale of the plane when
you bounded up silver stairs from the tarmac seemed like
story-book magic. in the 1950's, flying from San Francisco to
Connecticut with my sisters and my mom, i realized something was wrong: 'hey, Ma! there's smoke coming out of the
engine! there's flames!' we swooped down into O'Hare like a
wounded gull. i wasn't afraid, after all i'd saved us by spotting
the smoke. now all that's changed, all that little boy turn-on.
i loathe planes. they pack you in like sheep to the slaughter,
the seats can barely fit our bloated butts. the neck cramps,
insidious farting and used-up air is enough to make you want
to murder someone. meanwhile, there's no free anything to
drink or eat. ok. i admit that i like the take-offs and landings.
i like watching streets, cars and houses recede into monop-
oly pieces. i like the new stewardesses and (gay) stewards

who aren't Hollywood hot anymore and have saggy old-bra
breasts, age lines, thinning hair and bad makeup. but that all
goes awry when i imagine crashing into shark water, or sky
scrapers, when i'd be forced to make friends with the idiots on
board just to survive. i wonder if i'd have what it takes, or if
they do. or will it be war. all this amuses me quietly. i feel my
brain-dead bimbo Mona Lisa smile smiling above it all, smiling at myself smiling at them. ah, the saintly witness, what a
joke! soon enough it all unravels and it's torture time. the tin
can trap becomes a nightmare. i try not to touch the fatty on
my left or work up a conversation with the good looking kid
who by chance takes the seat next to mine, baseball hat backwards, ear buds fending off inquiry. i try to sleep. i read until
my eyes ache. i hold off a piss. after a century of fetal cramps
and window squinting, the squawk box announces descent.
down, down, down as cotton wisps slither across the wings
and tiny house dots enlarge. the sun sparkles off man-made
lakes. the shadow jet hurtles across the relief map below like
a jack rabbit. the flaps rise, the wheels lower and we're down,
landed, safe, nudging up through the uncircumcised cock tube
as we hurry through, like sperm to the airport egg. that's
when it happens. that's when all hell breaks loose as we wait
for the sheep to yank out their bags from the over head and
get the-fuck-off the fucking plane. when i stand up, the curved
ceiling crooks my neck like a hanged man. it's then that i hear
it, the scream, the silent Edvard Munch scream that sucks
up the stale space in the cabin like a cyclone. we all hear it,
seething silently. the level of impatience is at code red. sweaty

necks, clenched jaws and beady eyes turn us into cattle just
prior to execution. that's when we're all alike. that's when we
cumulatively despise the out-to-sea asshole who can't locate his
carry-on, staring up at the stow-away like a stoner, oblivious
to the rage of the angry rats behind him who would strangle
him given half a chance. now i understand how frightening the
group impulse of a crowd in panic can be. i understand why
innocents get trampled to death. i would be first among them,
even as i smile my stewardess smile of phony acceptance.

BOURNE-D TO DEATH

i rent the movies, the Bourne movies, all three: Identity,
Supremacy, Ultimatum with The Bourne Erection soon to
follow. there he is, Matt Damon walking the walk, the Bourne
walk where fast and steady wins all races. i think Kiefer
Sutherland copied it whole: the walk, the look, the steady cam,
the speed freak jump cuts and paranoia. i watch in the afternoon, my bird food cereal on my lap and a pint of Cafe Bustelo
that will shuttle me to the shitter before half a cup is gone. i
shut off the TV mid-stream so i can get my art-for-the-day
underway, saving Jason for later. but here's the kicker: my
celluloid fantasy in perpetuity. as i stride down the hallway of
my railroad apartment i do the walk. the Jason Bourne/Matt
Damon bouncy heel walk, killer look, chin lowered, vigilant,
a laser beam from my forehead to a red dot targeting the sink

walk. sharp karate moves wash the dishes with a no-nonsense attack to the most insignificant detail. i don't even realize i'm doing this until i get it, me as Jason and i burst out laughing. my all-by-myself barking walrus, chin whiskers-in-the-air laugh at how incredibly not like Jason i am. i sneak a peek in the mirror only to catch the flouncy, over-conditioned stringy hair, no lips and 68-year-old yellow teeth that look asymmetrically filed down. there is no Hollywood here. no Matt Damon there. no Jason anywhere. just me. i do that a lot. leaving a movie theater i walk to my car, climb in and fire it up as if it was me up there on the silver screen. the after burn of the cinematic mind comes alive around me like the rainbow traces that follow the tails of sparrows in a 'Lucy in The Sky with Diamonds'-sky.

KILLING THE BIRTHDAY BALLOON

i'm not next-to-godliness obsessive, but i like my place to look clean, even if it isn't. what's more, i worry about the roaches coming back and about my cat snarfing up leftovers. she'll puke on my bedspread or in my shoes if she eats anything other than her chicken-'n-rice pellets. so i fingernail pick off the marinara spots, the curled onion peels and dead pasta that whoever cooked last night failed to wipe off the floor. i sponge the stove. i do the undone dishes. i vacuum. the thing

is, i don't go all out. my roommates are way more thorough
about cleaning than i am, it's just that they do it once in a
blue moon. i don't think they even notice mess the way i do.
but like i said, my work is spotty. i miss things. the surface of
the stove i wipe, but the grime in and around the burners i
leave untouched. in the bathroom i whisk about the bowl, but
miss stains on the tiles in back. in my room i vacuum under
the desk, but ignore the dust rats behind the piano. i make
the bed every morning. i punch up the pillows, but my room
mates? they don't do this stuff. on the other hand, they fuck a
lot more than i do. they're wiped out from it i suppose and if i
was fucking that much maybe my room would be a wreck too.
i berate myself for being an old auntie, tsk-tsking them in a
silent prayer that i'm setting an example, that they'll see that
i vacuumed the hallway and soon they'll do it too, right? they
don't. i rationalize 'ok, Rick, this sort of clean freak shit is a
priority for you, but it's not for them. it bothers you, it doesn't
bother them. so it's on your watch to get the job done.' then
again, who cares when the entire planet is on the ropes and
people are being slaughtered in Afganistan? a tidy apartment
is a blackhead on the ass of real life. which brings me to today
and the birthday balloon. i borrowed a big white balloon at
work from one birthday party and gave it to my roommate
who was having her own celebration in another part of the
restaurant. i figured you gotta have a fucking balloon on a day
like that. anyhow, she brought it home. it kissed the ceiling for
awhile, lost helium and descended to the floor where it slept
for weeks. i thought it would eventually turn into a rubber

scrotum and die, but it didn't. it retained enough gas to lie
around the house like a loser, useless and semi-flacid. because
it said 'Happy Birthday' in black magic marker, i hadn't the
heart to kill it until today as i was tidying up. there it was in
the living room, under a window, staring up at me as if to say
'you got the balls to do this or what?' i felt guilty, but i carried
it into the kitchen on one arm like a baby. i plucked a knife out
of the drainer and this is when it got weird. i shut my eyes.
yup, i shut my eyes and looked away, same as when the nurse
draws blood. it's not the pin prick, it's the sight of the needle
going into my vein that gives me the creeps. so i pinched the
balloon by it's scrawny chicken neck, closed my eyes, turned
my head and stabbed. 'POP!' it wasn't that loud. it was more
like a 'pip' and then it was over. i could swear it felt pain, as
if i heard a small cry. my heart sank. my lower lip trembled. i
plopped it on top of an empty pizza box in the pantry,
sad, abandoned and dead. maybe i was one of those hooded
executioners in a previous life time and this was my scaredy-
cat karma.

CAR WASHED

my car, the GrandAm my Mum bought used knowing she
would die and i would inherit it, is a filthy stinking mess. i
tune up the engine. i change the oil. the brakes and tires are
checked but the interior, the inside shell of my menstrual-red

Pontiac, is bad news. it's banged up and bent, the aerial is twisted like a raw nerve, the AC is unable to make up its hot- or cold-mind, the window on the driver's side can only be raised or lowered with a clothes line (my autobody pal said, 'it's '300 bucks or a rope job'), dust furs the dash, the back seat is torn loose from its moorings and crushed down to accommodate my piano, deflated Stop & Shop carry bags lie like discarded toilet paper on the back seat, the screw driver i use to pry open the lid on the gas tank peeks out from under- neath a jumper cable Putanesca, one of the fog lights is out of it's socket and rolls around like a fake eyeball and the whole interior reeks of garbage. 'don't you ever clean this wreck?' i'm asked. my excuse is the weather. if i wash it, it'll rain or snow, i'll lose the shine and the 15 bucks it cost to run it through. but today is cowboy clear and i've felt guilty long enough. i will drive to my favorite car wash in Brookline, pay the next-to-cheapest option, enjoy the ride-thru and tidy the fucker up. i'd rolled the passenger window down so i could get a breeze in the car and, as i pull in, i reach over to wind it back up and at the same time pay the dude collecting at the gate, a gay-frenzy multi-task. he sprays her down, fish hooks the front end, the car lurches forward and off we lumber. i know that the window on the driver's side will leak so i yank the ropes taut like a champ and that's when it happens, that's when i'm hit in the side of the face by soap and spray—hot soap, hot spray. what the fuck!? in closing the passenger window i'd actually lost it completely; it disappeared down the slot. soapy goo frosts me like a pearl neckless, a glue gun in the hands of the Terminator. i try to close the window but, like the driver's side, it's off track. the harder i hernia to lift it, the more it refuses, the more water and suds froth in and the more i'm fighting a Waterloo. a pool of green slime collects on the passenger seat like a toxic pond and i lose it, breaking into cascades of laughter. the spray, the wet, the slime, the entire gizmo is jerking off all over me and i'm deliriously happy. next up: wind tunnel—vaporizing hot air to blow dry soapy jiz. i press against the remaining shard of window so that it won't come flying out of its slit and slice me in the neck and then it's over. we're through the maze, my car and i, as we are regurgitated out the ass-end of the colonic machinery all sparkly and smiling. i round the bend and park next to the vacuum hose so i can suck out the ugliness, but i realize that i must look ridiculous, like the clown who stuck his finger in the socket, hair like Bozo, a failed wet t-shirt contestant. i shake my head. i fire up the vacuum and give liposuction only to realize that the grand dames of Brookline are peering at me with 50's disdain as they buff their Mercedes and Audi's all high and mighty about this gonzo freak show. i know now how valuable the fool is at court.

CHEW BACCA LAUREATE

why is it that i fail to notice or to look at people when they chew? i don't. i won't. it's too cud-like and unflattering. i imagine how i must appear chomping on a runny egg, or

spoofting bits of oyster cracker onto a table of startled customers like a dog, chops flibbering, spit flying. not a pretty
sight. at the movies i notice actors chew the way they've been
taught at drama school, as if there's nothing but soft air in
the mouth. 'i am pretending to eat but i still look fabulous.' at
brunch where the hangovers chow down, the gnashing that
coincides with mastication i ignore. i see eyes, beards, shorts,
legs, ass, but no chaw. nobody chews in my universe. i picture
other things, dirty things, hot behavior, but not chewing.
behind a Geisha fan i bat averted eyes.

FART QUEEN

i know. some do, some don't. or they say they don't, but they
do, don't they? right? everybody fart (is that an R.E.M.
song?). anyhow it is not who farts but who thinks they're
funny and who doesn't. my sisters do. my nieces and nephews
don't. my (German) roommate does. my co-workers don't. my
father did. my mother did not. she slapped me loud and hard
across the face in a Thai restaurant after i cut a string-of-
pearls oinker (i was in my 50's). she did not think it was funny,
except once when i blew a brown note into my cat Ralph's
face. Mum was sitting on the couch and peering over a magazine as i squatted and aimed artillery inches in front of his
little pink eraser. he squinted, edged a bit into the brown blizzard, wrinkled his nose and sniffed, as if reading tea leaves.

Mum lost it. she doubled over with tears of laughter. i got her. just that once. so i guess even with the proprietary, a fart can make you laugh. it is one of those rare unpredictable acts we humans are capable of. we never know, we can never predict what it will sound like, or how it will stink. like jazz, it improvises its own vocabulary. i don't think i'll ever get over it. armpit blats were funny when i was five. sour puffs in high school english were historical events. in the sickening incubation of an enclosed fuselage everyone is suspect and grim. in a noisy bar, egg and beer conspire to force you to the floor or out the door. in elevators you blame them on an infuriated friend. Holden Caulfield cut one in chapel and that was in a book you had to read. i doubt i will ever get over doing, hearing, talking about, waking up to these foul snorts out the dirty door. they keep the kid in all of us present and accounted for. embarrassed? well maybe, once, though it's more of a shit than a fart story. on the dance floor at Villa Victoria, Daisy, a black queen, asked if i wanted to do a bump. why not? a teensy pebble of coke won't make me crazy and maybe i'll transform into a dancin' fool. so i did it, right then and there and immediately had to go. had to go bad before i shit myself. there was only one unisex piss pot and this being an emergency i cut in line, squirreled in and locked the door. i knew how bad it was going to be. i'm not sure if it's the shit itself, the gas or the effect of cocaine on nostrils that does this, but i can assure you it is just The Worst Smell Ever and sure enough, the results were ungodly. i batted at the fumes to disperse them and planned on returning to Daisy and the hot

pump of the dance floor, but realized, as i exited (slamming
the door in hopes that it would kick back the smut smog) that
a line of 10 frantic queens were waiting to get in there and
bump themselves silly. uh oh. i ducked, arm in front of my
face like a Chicago mobster who doesn't want his picture in
the paper and bolted for the door just as les girls rushed in
and then almost immediately ricocheted back out in a fanfare
of shrieking, fanning noses, coughing and gasping for air. i'm
outed, flat out outed. i squirmed through to the exit and made
my way home, tail between rubber legs. the moral: shitting
and farting never amuses all the people all the time.

GOT PHYSICAL?

we all know where this leads: ye olde finger up ye olde
stovepipe. we think about it on the way there. will he forget?
would we remind him? does he look forward to it, or does he
resist? will there be a smudge spot left on the paper afterwards to be scraped up by an orderly? will he, this time, find
a broccoli-sized nub in there to be burned out, sliced up and
scare the be-jesus out of us? will it be time for that loathsome
unit, the black snake? trapped for days with nauseating gulps
of Gator Aid, CVS enemas and a nurse reminding us that
'the drugs are awesome.' you think about it, all of it, if time is
on your side or if it's not and you realize, as the clock winds
down, that these visits will increase. that bad news will begin

to happen to your body. that fear will intrude on sane reflection, that on a sunny day it might rain. so far i've been lucky
in the doctor/diagnosis department. for the last ten years
i've had the same primary with the same 'you're fine' salute.
he's thorough. he spends more time on me than the allotted
HMO hurry-up, he has seen me through minor worries and
reads me like a country doc. like the honest auto-mechanic
who gets the difference between silly and serious, my guy
never advocates procedures or drugs that won't heal or help.
sadly, he's been transferred to Florida. good for him, not
good for me. my most recent annual is with a new dude who
has, as President Obama might say, a 'funny name.' as soon
as he comes through the door to check me out in my reverse
blue-green house dress, my heart jumps. this guy drop-dead
resembles the phony interns i've seen on porn sites. the ones
who 'examine' their hot young patients, heart, lungs, glands,
only to eventually jerk them off into oblivion. the 'patients'
mildly resist until they let go all over the place. i'm doubly
in doubt about my new guy when i notice his long eyelashes
and borderline lisp. 'uh oh' i'm thinking, 'the prostate check
is gonna be weird.' he snaps on the rubber glove like Nurse
Ratched and is in and outta there like a mouse to the cheese.
whoa! the doc has skills. he wraps up the look-see, says i'm
in good shape and informs me that in one year's time he, like
my previous primary, will be moving on. i'll have to hunt and
peck another fella (or woman?) to do the probe based on a
name, a funny name.

WHERE DO YOU PUT IT?

your snot? you pick your nose at a stoplight and what do you
do? fling it out the window? rub it onto the steering wheel?
under the seat? paste 'em behind your legs, smudging in
layers of crust that read like tree rings, dating all deposits.
or on your sock. who's gonna look at your sock? on foot you
smear lamp posts, like insect sperm, glistening on an aluminum pole. when sick and the spew of phlegm is infinite and no
surface can retain it, you fill a grocery bag with little birds of
discarded tissue. rubber-cementy boogers are rolled into BB's
and flicked across the living room floor. hard fingernails of
nose shale drop like bark onto linoleum. what else? are you
a watcher? do you want to see how others do? yup. i do that.
a kid in chapel, in third grade, had one finger knuckle deep,
eyes glassy, as he withdrew a glob and pasted it as if with a
paintbrush across his school sweater, a diagonal tape worm
Pollock-ing a narrow filthy front. my next-door neighbor
threatened: 'i bet i can make you moo-oove.' 'no ya caa-an't'
'yes i caa-aan.' a perpetual snot river ran out of his nose, down
his upper lip and into an open mouth. green-yellow slugs.
he'd gob 'em up into a french twist, like cotton candy, raise it
over his head and that's when you ran, the boy at your heels
snorting his nose off. a friend in high school, shuffling up a
receiving line at a debutante party, flobbed an oyster onto the
exposed tit of the girl whose tiny Chinese hand he was shak-

ing. it landed like egg yolk and quivered as if wondering what to do with itself. her mom, all brisk Philadelphia efficiency, whisked out a hanky and dabbed the doo-doo off the boob. 'never you mind,' she might have said. my dad, squirming like a salmon against the current of grey flannel suits on their way to work, was fighting for a seat on the commuter rail. he harked back a flapjack of goo, collecting it in his throat and zinged a slo-mo parabola at the idiot running in front of him. the target clapped his hand on the back of his neck as if shot. Dad surged ahead, knees pumping and made his train. and then there's the pocket hanky conundrum. in college my East African roommate had grown up in Zanzibar. over there you press finger to nostril, close it off and fire your product onto the sidewalk, grass, tarmac, toilet, wastebasket or desert sand. he thought it unclean to save the dried deposits in a hanky. so i adopted his slingshot approach. i loved it. it made perfect sense, but it got me into trouble in Central Square. i was mid-snort, head down and didn't see the kid approaching, hand up for a high-five. friend, fan, who knows? what i do remember is that my ju ju flew like a mortar onto his brand new Converse All-Star. i will never learn. i am, as the girls at Doyle's say: 'gross.'

TITS OR BOOBS?

what d' ya call 'em? girls prefer boobs. guys, tits. breasts sound too clinical, too sibilant. knockers are dated. bosoms

are faux poetic and get stuck in the mouth when said. 'boobs'
sounds dumb, like water grenades, demeaning in a goofy way.
and tits are what? smaller? more perky, more upright, hard
nippled? on odd occasions i take a sampling, a census. 'tits' or
'boobs?' i ask. of course there's a thousand Chaucerian options
i could look up. i could Google tits to see what's en vogue, but
i don't. it's all tits all the time far as i'm concerned. how about
you? tits or boobs? you already know, don't ya? shout it out.

HERPES

was the name of Chet and Billie's cat. he was orange and yellow,
like the sore without the pus. i think Chet had the stigmata on
his cock and so kitty got honored with the diagnosis. Kelly had
it on her lip, upper right. in her yearbook picture she did the
one-finger rescue, just so. her classmates duplicated the gesture
in support. 10's of pretty girls with cocked head and forefinger on the upper right smiley lip just so. we always knew who
her boyfriends were because they all had the same burnt bacon
scab in same spot. an Irish girl at work had it so bad her entire
mouth was Cajun black. i have one, mid-upper. it cracks open at
gigs and bleeds a trickle when i hit the mike in an extravagant
emotional moment. the thing is, herpes ain't AIDS so we kinda
laugh it off, but i wonder about the origins, the ontology. who
gives it to us? was it a deep french kiss in Prague? foul drinking
water from an over-shared bottle? a nefarious coke-addled blow

job? it ID's you, herpes, as if to indicate and tag an overactive, dirty sex life (if there is such a thing). who wouldn't want that, the scab badge of courage? at some point Lysine softened the symptoms. an occasional thumper pulsing on my upper lip reminds me of an old friend, but he never materializes. he is a he, isn't he? Mr. Herpes with a South Park address. a particularly man-triggered flag. what would constitute a female STD? warts? warts down there? i dunno. thank god i rarely 'show' these days.

WORD SNOB

it's small change, my cringe reaction to catch-all phrases. still, i loathe 'it's all good' as a flipping coin inclined to dispel any annoyance. lately it's been replaced with 'no worries,' EVERYBODY says 'no worries.' who started this? how did it take hold? didn't we all hate 'don't worry, be happy' as bumper sticker easy-as-pie pablum even though it originated with Meher Baba and stood on solid guru ground? the 'no worries' slight-of-hand as an upbeat 'whatever' curls the neck hair. within the last couple of years 'real quick' is all over the sidewalk, a no-problem, wait-a-sec, snap-your-fingers insta-solution to any troubling knot in the day will be taken care of 'real quick.' it's not even the the absentee 'ly' that bothers me so much as the fact that everyone i know, friends and not-friends use it. this may be part of the wait-

ress-hears-too-many-verbal-shortcuts syndrome. lastly, and
this is totally a waitress complaint and leaks primarily from
girls, is 'thank yeeeew'—the 'eew' being drawn out in a small
'o'-shaped mouth and held onto for dear life. nasal and obnoxious and never ending. like fingernails on the blackboard. why
this stuff plugs me in so disastrously i cannot fathom. like a
filthy habit, i can't give it up.

MUSEUM SCAN

went to the MFA yesterday to see the Degas nude exhibit.
hurtled through, impatiently weary became weary of
looking at women's backs and bath tubs. i was aware, however,
that i was scoping out the boys. those alone, with girlfriends,
or moms and dads. they would be lost or pretending to be
lost in a painting as i was lost in them. museums are weird.
the sweat of the artist hung convincingly, although dryly
it seemed, on careful walls when i would prefer to live with
them in my house—an impossibility given the price tag on
the long dead. thus the turmoil and joy of the artist winds
up on perfect walls for all of us to visit. a good thing i guess,
even if still not cheap. $20-a-pop for a senior. how reverently
quiet the slow-moving line was around the exhibit. tense
eyebrows, flickering looks, attempts at 'getting' what they see.
like myself, i presume they imagine the painter zeroing in on
the whore in the tub, a boner boning out of his 19th-century

flouncy drawers, many thoughts zinging around in his brain as he cuts sharp dark lines on the edge of a calf, a torso, a tit. staring at her with respect and desire. he must be, right? as i stare with equal respect at the boy, slightly behind his father, who is partly bored, elsewhere in his head, or vaguely aware of the stranger nearby who is staring at him with the intensity of a bird dog.

CHIEF SPLINTER-IN-FOOT

like everyone else in town, i caught the flu. i fought back, got the shot, washed my hands like Howard Hughes, and brought the gift the non-sick give to the sick: you have it. i don't. hardy har-har-har—basking in one's tenuous knock-on-wood health. fake out, Berlin, you got it. the slope slipped and there i was, aching in every joint, too weak to get out of bed and with enough of a cough to throw my back out. it happened at Stop & Shop. i stopped to shop, wheeled a cart out of the queue and felt like i'd been shot in the ass. i let out a scream, soundless, like a cat getting a final solution shot. i got what i needed and drove home. it hurt like hell. i laid on an ice pack and stretched my old lady yoga positions, but it only got worse. i could have called my go-to neuromuscular guy, but he lives in Watertown and i didn't want to make the trip or thin the wallet, so i booked a massage AND a chiropractor here in the 'hood. had my doubts about the chiro (fear of the yank-n-twist), but decided to throw the kitchen sink at my back: an

all out war. i almost missed my first appointment and in the
frenzy to be on time, shoved a splinter into the ball of my foot
(the floor in our apartment is wood. my office chair, rolling
between two computers, chews it to bits, leaving porcupine
arrows primed to fire into exposed feet). i plucked it out (a
five-inch dart) but in my impatience, left a pin-point piece
under the dermis. i hobbled to the lady chiro and, two hours
later, saw the rub-down dude. he knew his shit, but talked
about himself non-stop, as if he had a vanity mirror attached
to a harmonica holder so he could admire his fabulousness
at all times. dude loves the dude. my back improved but the
splinter was still in there. buried. i couldn't see it so i called
my doc and she sent me to Brigham and Women's for an
ultra-sound (was i pregnant? would i see a little splinter-ette
squirming around in there with a beating heart?). a dwarf
nurse, all business, located the pin point. 'see a podiatrist and
get it cut out asap,' she said. a foot doc in Chestnut Hill did
an x-ray but couldn't see anything. he wanted to check the
ultra, but they wouldn't allow him to download the image
(would i sue them over a splinter-ette?), so i had to drive back
to Brigham, collect the evidence and return to Chestnut Hill
before the podiatrist left for the day. he read the tea leaves
and advised: a) do nothing or b) have surgery. i pictured my
dot salmon squiggling up a vein, into my heart and piercing
the aorta, or becoming infected, requiring amputation and
a roller skate prosthetic. i knew this would keep me out of
work (no paid leave), so i opted for the knife. they rolled me in,
anesthesia in a hang bag, but i have no memory of it, of being

there or getting wheeled out. something about a mind-eraser drug added to the drug cocktail. the splinter was excised and my foot bandaged. they gave me crutches, a boot and a script for Percodan. i lived on my couch, watched 10,000 movies and boycotted the Behan. when it began to throb, i swallowed a Perc, two Aleves and smoked a hit of pot. i slept on my brand-new, stiff-but-squooshy Bob-o-Pedic (bought on the advice of Shamus who, with back problems of his own, insisted that i 'get a real mattress.' my futon is a limp-dick, 20-year-old snot rag). excluding the doctor, i'm closing in on a g-note from one girly cough and a splinter-ette. the boot makes me walk like a drag queen with a broken high heel—da-DUM, da-DUM—a list-n-twist to one side potentially re-injuring my back (no end to the dark dominoes). i wonder, if i was a dog, or in my 90's would i think this was it? unending, perpetual body break-down? then the blizzard hit.

GANDALF'S GOLDEN SHOWER

after the Hobbit, i have to piss. i'd held it in not wanting to miss one second of the five armies. a kid, a 9-year-old, takes the urinal next to mine. i don't look over. it ain't proper, but out of the corner of my eye i realize that he turned to look up at me. then back to his business. pause. then back to look up at me, mouth agape. i get it. with my Gandalf the Grey stringy hair he thinks i'm him, the great wizard, pissing next to

him. he really does. i want to give him a wink, but that would
be unwise. i do say, in my best bellowing Ian McKellen brit:
'SHOW ME THE MEANING OF HASTE, BOY!' to no one
in particular. it's loud. bounces off the men's room tiles.
i picture it. the kid rushes back to his parents: 'Mom! Dad!
Gandalf was going pee right next to me in there! i swear!' had
our places been reversed in years i would have thought exactly
the same thing.

LOL AND OBIT-A-PHOBIA

i talk to myself. i work things out, laugh through my never-let-
up-life's binoculars. driving to work listening to NPR comment
on the news i remark, like a stuffy British matron: 'Oh dear.
Oh really? Is that so?' pulling in my chin, wrinkling it up,
lower lip behind upper front teeth. tuning-in to classic rock/
pop hits at work, i punch a drag queen's mimed vibrato button.
that as-if-i'm-singing up and down jaw like a false-teeth joke
chatterer at crack speed: uh uh uh uh uh. i am the funniest
person alive. of course no one else gets it. who cares? a few
decades back they probably would have put me away, slobbering in a straight jacket. i rehearse conversations with a 'person
of interest,' imagining the seductive result. it flops onto the
cutting room floor, meaningful sentences ground underfoot, a
verbal belly flop. again i bust a gut. i am my perfect nonjudg-
mental comedic audience. there is always a crowd of me when

i yap with my bad self. the imagined obit, or words spoken
at my rained-on funeral: 'none of us could ever forget Rick's
beloved_____ (fill in the blank).' i hope to Christ no
one writes or uses that phrase when i'm on the slab. there i go
again, trying it out. 'how can any of us forget Berlin's beloved
fuck doll?'

CLOSE CALLS THAT I CAN REMEMBER: TOBOGGAN AND SPEAR

ten. a hill outside our front door in Philly spilled down past an
old ice-house and a giant stump of a tree with a brass plaque:
'this tree was alive when Ben Franklin lived in Philadelphia.'
the tree looked like Methuselah. we'd toboggan downhill
just to the right of the ice house. a slight incline chafed the
toboggan to a stop. i sat up front, arms around knees, racing towards a thicket. we hit a bump, lifted off the ground
and landed with a thud at a dead stop. a needle shard of dead
branch quivered one inch from my eyeball like an accusing
finger. the breath went out of my body. i turned and looked at
the kid behind me, his eyes wide in horror.

SHARK AND BARRACUDA

fourteen. zits like pizza. family trip to Bermuda. 'had feelings for' this green-eyed kid from Oklahoma. long looks,
no action. we took a walk down a scrabbly broken sea shell
beach and climbed a coral cliff. when we got to the top we
discovered a 100-foot-deep, ¾-round rough-sided, open coral
cylinder that ended in a turquoise slosh of ocean, shimmering in the heat. my show-off idea was to scale down with my
friend and swim in the pretty water. i inched 10 feet below
the lip when i spotted a fin circling and a school of had-to-be
barracuda (we'd been warned they were all over the island). i
froze, hanging by fingernails. my friend ran for help and the
handsome prince lifeguard appeared above, lowered himself
delicately, grabbed my forearm and hauled me to safety. i felt
like a fool, but somehow knew i'd do stupid over and over
again in romance land.

TIN CAN AND CHERRY BOMB

twenty. on tour with my Yale singing group. in stilted love
with one of the just-joined freshmen. pit stop at my house in
Philly. i decide to set off a cherry bomb under a can of dog
food. like this was a cool idea? i set the cherry, lit it with the
can over it, walked away and BANG! i threw my arms up—an
automatic reaction—forearm in front of face. the top of the

can shot off like a tiny tin frisbee cutting a fat red blood smile on my arm, three inches wide and down to muscle. could have lost an eye.

SHOTGUN AND GAS STATION

twenty-three. my friend Lilian and i drove her black MG Midget cross country. needle below empty, heading towards Vegas, sky exploding with stars. up ahead slept a rusty gas station 'n snack-shack. no neon. no light. no one about. we limped in and knocked on the screen door. nada. we had to fill her up. wanted to hit Vegas (no scorpions in desert sleeping bags). i clanked the nozzle loose and gurgled gas into the Midget. i was about to slither a sawbuck under the door when i heard it: the bright double pump of a shotgun being cocked. 'what the FUCK are ya doin' pumpin' MY gas into your car, asshole?' (muzzle pointed six inches from my forehead). 'ah... hmmm...let me explain' as fast as i could talk. he held the gun at my head for ten infinitely long seconds before lowering it. we paid double. the dude could have dug us a shallow grave. no one knew where we were. would have ended my brilliant career then and there.

UMBRELLA AND A SIXTEEN WHEELER

thirty-four. Luna playing a big room off a highway on Revere Beach. big stage, big lights, big sound, big crowd, big hair. coke insinuating its bad self into our amped-up lives. dealers in the dressing room: it was that kind of gig, that kind of band. i crossed the highway to grab a clam roll. it was raining, hard horizontal bullets. my umbrella offered flimsy protection. heading back to the club i teetered on the medial strip, balancing and waiting for the oncoming traffic to clear. i held the umbrella as a shield—to 'read' traffic through black silk skin. looked ok. no blurry headlights. as i took a step onto the asphalt. the umbrella was ripped out of my hands by a sixteen wheeler doing 60 mph. fucked up my 80's hairdo.

AND ANOTHER THING...

to flush or not to flush? as for me, i flush because i don't get it. saving water is the point, right? but every time i have to go and there it is: yellow bubbles and a corsage of submerged toilet paper, i flush. i don't want the splashy-splashy on my ass if i'm sitting down. i don't want it on my shins if i'm standing. i appreciate the footprint gesture and i worry: am i over-reactively squeamish? i don't think so. i don't know anyone (though i've never asked) who wants piss on their ass or legs (i know, there are exceptions). and i'd even be ok with a Yoko Ono camera 'Bottoms' snapshot. that's art. piss on legs: not art. not for me. i will seethe and add to the footprint.

GARGLING SOAP: THE RECIPE

one bottle of Dr. Bronner's, brand new. one shower stall. one stinky naked body in a rush to get it over with and get to work on time. flip cap open and squeeze bottle into hand. nothing. squeeze again. Prophylactic, un-peeled dental dam flap refuses the discharge. unscrew cap. tweeze off flap with fingernail pliers. fingernails too short. brain storm: bite edge of flap with teeth. peel off flap. squeeze bottle with happy delight. engorge mouth with soap. try not to puke. spit, spit, spit it out. mouth under nozzle. eat bread. gulp water. wait seven hours until it goes away. realize you are a fucking idiot.

A REAR-END AND AN ASSHOLE

it's the friday before the JP Music Festival. returning to the hood with fifth annual t-shirts all happy and new in the back of my car, driving with an easy smile. in a carefree mood, taking my homing pigeon route from Somerville to the J-Way, i nose into the circle that slips under the overpass and inch up

onto the BU bridge, a never-ending clusterfuck where two
lanes collide and every car seems to want the slot not taken.
i'm still in naïve oblivion until this idiot tries to pass me on
the right and jumps the line. blood boils. no fucking way am
i going to let this no-manners shit-head squeak past me. but
he guns it and purrs in ahead as if he gets away with this all
the time. i lean on my high-pitched girly horn with no cred:
a tiny, doll-voice warning, as if to say: 'please, sir. would you
mind? (i think) i have the right of way.' more embarrassing
than scary. i lower my window and start yelling indecipher-
able nonsense at the cocksucker, rattling a saber-fisted middle
finger as effective as my horn. i can see him laughing. i can
see his baby blue button-down shirt and knotted tie, his man-
icured nail-job, shoes shined in a CEO corridor (no tip). this
guy may not be a one percenter but he makes enough dough
to own this fucking Audi and is gloating about his wise-guy
maneuver. then he brakes. right there on the bridge. hard and
fast. i slam on mine, i hear the squeal of rubber as i shiver
and stop less than an inch from his back bumper. he waits. he
waits some more. i think he's really pleased with himself. he
played me. again. i learn later (why don't i know these things?)
that he was doing it on purpose. trying to get me to rear-end
his car. that had i hit him from behind the law would say it
was my fault. his asshole move resulting in a) front-end damage to my car; b) my insurance going up, again; c) the t-shirts
getting mangled; d) a serious delay to all the shit i had yet
to do in prep for the festival and worst of all; e) having to eat
shit in front of this smart aleck in his precise, $400 suit. i pray

that there's a dank basement in 50 shades of hell waiting for him where he's getting dildo-jammed by an S&M contessa.

MR MAGOO

how is it that way too often i spot bizarre behavior in the act without looking for it? case(s) in point: 1) open one eye to see what time it is during meditation. outside my window a seagull lurches up and down in embarrassed flight, losing, then regaining altitude. flickering out of its ass feathers is strip of mylar a half inch wide, five feet long, whipping and flapping like a kite tail as if a mylar terrorist is trying to shove him off course. if i hadn't cracked a look at the clock i would have missed the whole scene; 2) up to pee at three AM i notice on the roof of the Northeastern dorm across from my room at the Piano Factory a chick with thigh high stiletto boots standing like a Valkyrie above a naked dude, on his back, legs up over his head. WHACK! she smacks his bare ass. looks down, convinced that this is what he wants. WHACK! she does him again. the crack of the slap rockets across the parking lot. i am dumbfounded, and cannot stop staring; 3) same location, weeks later, this time in the splinter of a 'backyard' behind the dorm, the frat boys have installed a swimming pool hot tub. a round job four feet high and bubbling with filthy froth. a late night party dream tub. my ping pong ball-sized bladder wakes me up. i hear giggling. curiosity walks me to the window. dude encourages date into the froth. she's reluctant, but it's 40 degrees out and the steamy bubbly is an offer she can't refuse. they slide into the tub, unsteady martinis in hand, arms around shoulders, partially submerged. he drinks. she drinks. and then, gently but with a sure hand, he guides her head under the surface and towards a soon-to-be pray-to-god money slurp 'n swallow. she burps up, gasping for breath. tries again, under water longer this time. he looks like Mr. Wish-cum-true until she busts the surface like an orca and spews vomit all over his face. now it's his turn. the sequel: vomit II. i am not some perv with binoculars looking to score a voyeur hit, i swear, but this shit happens to me a lot, blink, blink...

ALONG CAME A

spider. like an old lady standing on a chair with her dress hiked up over her knees—a mouse squirreling underfoot—i totally freak. ok. i like spiderMAN (Andrew Garfield's perfect ass in a spidey suit) but i've never met an itsy bitsy spider i didn't want to crush into unrecognizable parts. my personal Buddha takes a back seat to psychopathy on this one. case in point: got two new kittens. i feed them separately. it's time for new water in their happy bowl. as i fill it up, a towering brown 'n yellow creature skitters into the aluminum sink all spikey-legged and ferocious. i'm in Mirkwood Forest without a ring of invisibility (in the theater i covered my eyes). the bastard's legs are speed freak nimble. it wants to bite me i'm sure. i go into brain lock and dump kitty water from the bowl onto his tap-tap-tappy daddy long legs. this guy is at least two inches in diameter and an inch-plus tall. he is not deterred by kitty water, not one bit. he darts at me like he's on spider skates. i twist the spigot, yank it to 'hot' and spray the thing until he is gradually forced into and down the drain. i see his legs claw-ing for dear life—tick tick tick, pincers on high alert. i imag-ine i can see his 'face' grimace in pain. i let the steaming spray continue for long minutes until he is entirely, hopefully dead and gone. later i look up brown 'n yellow spiders on Google. they are house spiders and completely harmless. chalk one up for the Nazi in my Berlin DNA.

PANIC IN MOUSE PARK (JAMES JOYCE STYLE)

in the heat of the late afternoon in the midst of sorting out 10,000 idiotic details a) with Discmakers for our new Badville EP and b) with CD Baby so that the master that Bob did for us gets properly uploaded on iTunes, i'm on the phone at least seven times with both companies even though they're the same company and each time i think i have it all sorted out i hit another snag on another link page and have to call again and wait because the outgoing robot message keeps repeating:

'we are very busy with calls at this time and we'll get to you in X minutes.' and i go through this over and over again just as my computer screen lights up to warn me that the batteries on my mouse are low and i'd better jump on it or i'll be fucked and a text comes in from work to say they want me in there early and the kitties are staring up at me because it's feed time and the clock is running out on all this as i spill the batteries from my fireplace slim jim closet onto my desk, totally not sure which ones are good and which ones are dead because i'd popped the old ones out of my mouse to replace them in the same spot where the new ones are residing, glasses on, glasses off to locate a good one as the thermometer in my head climbs higher and higher because no matter which set of batteries i shove in the remote (and by the way where are the old-school mice i used to have lying around?! no amount of standing on a chair in my party closet will turn up an old-school mouse) the mouse still doesn't work and my computer screen is frozen. glasses on, glasses off, glasses misplaced and now it's getting later and closer to D-Day for getting the cats fed and getting pretty for work and it's time to call Applecare but i can't access my address book because my mouse isn't active and there's no cursor but wait, the Applecare number's in my iPhone so i make the call, more robot outgoing messages and someone answers to direct my call and can i please give her the serial number of my iMac? and i yell at her no, i can't do that because my mouse isn't working and my screen is locked and WHAT THE FUCK!!! i'm screaming at her and she is calm like a shrink facing down a madman 'what is your email

address?' and i give it to her and that does the trick. i can hear
her smiling as my blood is reaching the boiling point and i
get Jake or Jonah or Puck or some handsome-voiced kid on
the phone and run the whole megillah down all over again
for him and he says he'll be able to help he understands how
frustrating this must be for me (my filthy language over the
phone confirming this), so we try to shut down and re-start
the iMac holding down option/control which i do and nothing
changes but then he tells me that i missed two additional and
essential keys that need to be held down at the same time as
command/option and i'm hoping that maybe we're close on
this shit and so i do the hold down of all four keys and it
takes a century for the fucking iMac to re-boot and still no
mousey-wousey and no cursor arrow and i suggest could Jake
or Jonah or Puck stay on the line while i run across the street
to the the Bodega in my socks and get new batteries to be
sure they are actually new and he says 'sure' and i can hear
him kinda laughing while my panic has by now upped full
throttle and i do it, i am the Flash and i zing across Centre St.
and buy four good batteries and he is amazed at how quickly
i get this done (what he pictures in terms of where i live and
what my world must look like to him i can only imagine) he
has to have heard the spoons on the cat food plates that i was
doling out while the re-boot was taking its own sweet time,
right? to him i am an insane person but who knows? who
cares? i jam the two new coppery Duracells into the
mouse's back and try it again and FUCK! it still doesn't work
and he's looking at some graphic at Applecare, a blueprint

graphic of mice and realizes that there's a miniature nipple
thing just inside the lip of the mouse where i'd put the batteries which at the exact same time i had noticed myself AS he
was explaining it to me and i flick it north or south and a tiny
green LED lights up and i snap the flat tin piece back in place
and DAMN! it works and I'm in business and i say out loud
'motherFUCKER! panic is not a good place to make decisions
from,' and he is laughing and says he concurs and that i was
fun, funny to talk to and i finish up the Dropbox transfer of
song masters for iTunes and hit the blazing shower and make
it a less-than-normal meditation and the cats are sleepy again
in their food coma and i storm off to work and get there just
in time and my God, it took what? less than an hour to go
from massive freak-attack to total nerve calm and maybe i
noticed that while it was all going down in the needle center
of my ten-thousand-swarming-hornets panic i was, strangely,
at peace and watching the whole miserable ridiculous episode
from a planet far far away.

BEHIND THE FAN

downstairs at Brandy's ('The Place Where Friends Are
Made') in Allston. warming up in the backstage corridor for
an Orchestra Luna gig, next to the ice machine. just inside the
door is a Miro arrangement of dog shit. dog must have been
spinning and dropping simultaneously. the coat hanger used

to keep the door ajar jiggles and a small hand, black finger-nails, appears. a girl. a short girl, toothpick thin, long straight inky black hair. make-up inspired by the Addams Family. she wriggles in. her voice is deep in her chest, low and guttural. 'aaarrr eeyew in thee Orchestra Luna?' 'yes.' 'what is eeyor name please? ' 'Rick.' 'Reek?' 'yes. what's yours?' 'what!?' 'what's your name?' 'wait!' hands up, stop-in-the-name-of-love signal, lowering of eyebrows. 'wait! (a noir secret to be imparted) my name ees...MALAHGRO...Malahgro. please repeat. Ma...lahg...RO!' 'Malahgro.' 'no! wait!...Ma...' 'Ma...' 'lahg...' 'lahg...' 'ro.' 'ro.' 'RO!' 'ro.' ' yes.' 'where do you live? 'upstairs.' 'oh.' 'WAIT! please! (finger to lips) i am going now. goodbye.' 'goodbye.'

¶

ABOUT THE AUTHOR

Rick Berlin is a Boston-based singer-songwriter, formerly the frontman of Orchestra Luna, Berlin Aircraft, Rick Berlin: The Movie, and The Shelly Winters Project.

His discography includes:

Rick Berlin w/ THE NICKEL & DIME BAND
ALWAYS ON INSANE
WHEN WE WERE KIDS
BADVILLE
(THE COURAGE OF THE LONELY 2017 release)

Rick Berlin ('solo')
HALF IN THE BAG (w players) (unreleased)
RICK BERLIN LIVE@JACQUES
ME & VAN GOGH
OLD STAG (w/ string quartet)
PAPER AIRPLANE (w/ 'ringer' band)

The Shelley Winters Project
EP
I HATE EVERYTHING BUT YOU
FORCED 2 SWALLOW
CATHEDRAL (unreleased)

Rick Berlin The Movie
RATED: FOREIGN (unreleased)
ROME IS BURNING (unreleased)

Berlin Airlift
BERLIN AIRLIFT
PROFESSIONALLY DAMAGED

Orchestra Luna
ORCHESTRA LUNA

Other Works by Rick include *The Kingdom: a Musical, Go for It Girl: A Queer Travelogue,* and *Armchair General: a Fictional Autobiography of Dick and Jane,* all published on his website www.berlinrick.com.

CPSIA information can be obtained
at www.ICGtesting.com
Printed in the USA
FSOW01n0152131216
28487FS